Preparing to Teach Social Studies for Social Justice

Becoming a Renegade

Ruchi Agarwal-Rangnath
Alison G. Dover
Nick Henning

Foreword by Rick Ayers

TEACHERS COLLEGE PRESS
TEACHERS COLLEGE | COLUMBIA UNIVERSITY
NEW YORK AND LONDON

Published by Teachers College Press, 1234 Amsterdam Avenue, New York, NY 10027

Cover painting by Luis-Genaro Garcia. Cover design by Laura Duffy Design.

Library of Congress Cataloging-in-Publication Data is available at loc.gov

ISBN 978-0-8077-5766-6 (paper)
ISBN 978-0-8077-7477-9 (ebook)

Printed on acid-free paper
Manufactured in the United States of America

23 22 21 20 19 18 17 16 8 7 6 5 4 3 2 1

Contents

Foreword

Today, education content and performance standards are accepted as the common sense, everyday reality of schooling. And who would not want some kind of accountability, some sort of coherence in what is taught in our schools? But we must understand that the standards we live with today, from No Child Left Behind to the Common Core, did not just drop from the sky. They are a specific product of the culture wars that rocked education in the 1980s, and those confrontations were themselves the consequence of the explosion of liberatory initiatives that came with the Black Power and anti-colonial and feminist struggles of the 1960s and 1970s.

Starting with E. D. Hirsh's *Cultural Literacy: What Every American Needs to Know*, William Bennett's *The De-Valuing of America*, and reports such as *A Nation at Risk*, conservatives unleashed a counter-wave of patriotic core knowledge rhetoric. Under the guise of making schooling more rigorous and consistent, wealthy foundations and government commissions sought to declare, from the top, what knowledge was worth acquiring.

Over the last 20 years, large foundations have set themselves up as arbiters of education policy. Money talks, and billionaires such as Gates and Walton, sitting on obscene amounts of money, have effectively installed themselves as Chief Education Officers. Taking the broad view, we can see that this wealth is the result of our failure to tax them adequately. Such excess wealth is always socially generated and must therefore be taxed as the start of some kind of collective, democratic process to decide how to spend it. With the tax system decimated, wealthy individuals hold the cash and decide educational policies with scant input from communities, parents and students, teachers, or education scholars. We can best understand the mania for standards in that context. Ultimately, as the authors point out, such policies (under whatever name) tend to press for a dominant pattern of social studies instruction characterized by text-oriented, whole-group, teacher-centered approaches aimed toward the transmission of "factual" information. Thus the form and content of such pedagogy reinforces the master narrative of Euro-American dominance.

In Communication Arts and Sciences, the small school I was part of at Berkeley High School, we had a unique response to the flood of new standards in the late 1990s. Instead of resisting standards, we decided to add new, locally generated standards of our own. Our "Social Justice Standards" articulated a pedagogy founded on democracy, on support for public space, on self-awareness and social literacy, on collective action, and on the power of imagination and creativity. These standards were never blessed by the state, but we felt better to be appropriating this narrative for our own purposes.

What we did not bother to do, what we did not have the expansive vision to do, was to examine how other social justice teachers across the country were responding to the "standards movement." That is where Agarwal-Rangnath, Dover, and Henning's important book comes in. After reviewing various adaptations and responses to standards, the authors offer extensive and specific suggestions for secondary social studies teachers seeking to pursue a social justice agenda within the current context. Such teachers approach curriculum and pedagogy from an engaged, even passionate, commitment to their students. They bring to the relationship not just a disembodied transmission of information, but what Valenzuela calls *cariño*, a personal connection. For social justice teachers also act as mentors, supporters, and allies of their students—a relationship of solidarity. They don't just propose a line, even a progressive line. They help students to experience social analysis, to own and develop their own investigations, and to draw their own conclusions. Such students are not simply prepared to fit into the dysfunctional society as it is, but are empowered to make a world that they need, one that is a place for their communities to thrive.

So many things are right about the approach of this book. First, it focuses on the classroom and actual practice. Too often, our critical responses to problematic policies are to advance polemics and critiques. But sites in which these struggles matter most immediately are in the classrooms themselves, in the way teachers respond and pursue their work. These are teachers who are working hard to teach within the school system, and even under the Common Core standards, to advance social justice agendas.

Moreover, this response evokes an important caveat we must keep in mind during contemporary policy debates: There was never a "good old days" in education. Before standards, we did not have a golden age of creative, generative, inquiry based community education. Schools have always been zones of contention—between the authoritarian impulse of power on the one hand and the agitation and practice of democracy on the other. It's good to criticize problems with the current iteration of top-down standards and especially testing regimes, but let's remember that the struggle for social justice is just that, a struggle between different forces. We do our work in that liminal space, in the dynamic tension, in the dialectical struggle between classes and interests.

In the late 1960s Neil Postman described good teaching as a "subversive activity." From the beginning of schooling, educators have had to defy, undermine, evade, and bypass the mandates from above in order to serve their students and to be allies to their communities. *Preparing to Teach Social Studies for Social Justice: Becoming a Renegade* is a crucial tool to help teachers to do just that. What is at stake here is democratic education and democracy itself. That is the good fight of today.

—Rick Ayers

Acknowledgments

The writing of this book has been an incredible journey for us. We are especially grateful for all of the teachers who contributed to this book; Amelie, Brian, Carolina, David, Dawn, Eran, Isabel, Jared, Jennifer, Katy, Laura, Lindsay, Liz, Melissa, Michael, Nicole, Prentice, Rory, Sarah, and Tom. Without your fearless work and letters to fellow teachers, this book would not be possible. Your stories, lessons, and commitment to change give us hope and inspiration.

We are also deeply appreciative to the many close colleagues who supported our work. Thank you Rick Ayers, Kevin Kumashiro, Christine Sleeter, Brian Schultz, Bill Bigelow, Tyrone Howard, and Celia Oyler. Your words and actions of support encourage us to see this project as an important contribution to the field of social studies and social justice teaching.

As we all met somewhat serendipitously through events associated with the National Association of Multicultural Education (NAME), the American Educational Research Association (AERA), and the California chapter of NAME (CA-NAME), we feel grateful for having a community of like-minded educators with whom to engage in this work.

We also owe a debt of gratitude to Jean Ward, our editor, for providing us with guidance every step of the way. Your insight was invaluable. Thank you for your helpful and detailed feedback and believing in this project. We are also appreciative for the many others at TC Press who helped bring this book to print. Thank you Noelle de la Paz, Karl Nyberg, Vinolia Fernando, and the others at TC Press. For our wonderful cover art, we thank Luis-Genaro Garcia, an inspiring teacher, artist, doctoral student, and friend for contributing his painting, "El Estudiante".

And last, but not least, we are so grateful for the support we received from our family. Thank you to our partners, Praveen, Maria, and Tony; our children, Milan, Aahna, Joaquin, Aimara, Corabella, and Alia; and our parents, Rekha, Naresh, Linda, Bruce, Abby, Claudia, and Cliff. We are inspired by your example, your curiosity, and your belief in possibility. Dear children, our greatest hope is that you experience a lifetime of teachers as creative, passionate, and justice-oriented as the ones you will meet here.

We live in a day where great challenges face our schools and communities. The teachers presented in this book and their commitment to social justice provide us with the belief that change is possible. That belief nourishes and sustains us, and we hope that others find as much inspiration in the reading of this book as we did in the writing of it.

Part I

CONTEXT MATTERS: TEACHING SOCIAL STUDIES FOR SOCIAL JUSTICE IN THE COMMON CORE ERA

Contemporary approaches to teaching social studies for social justice draw on a robust foundation of justice-oriented educational traditions. In this Part, we examine the conceptual roots of teaching for social justice and the tensions inherent in teaching for social justice within an increasingly accountability-driven educational system. Our discussion traces the history of social studies standards and how they impact justice-oriented teachers. Next, we introduce readers to the 20 visionary, justice-oriented social studies teachers whose voices and experiences inform this volume, examining the multiple ways they are responding strategically to the influence of standards in their schools and classrooms.

CHAPTER 1

Introduction

> Implementing a social justice driven curriculum was more difficult than anticipated. My middle school students were curious and wanted to know about the world around them. They asked questions about inequality and race in Chicago especially during the 2008 election. They wanted to know why they saw more homelessness in their neighborhood. All of a sudden, I was flustered. How could I focus on these issues when I had to get through a jam packed curriculum from World War I to the War on Terror and be sure to cover most of the Illinois State Board of Education standards for middle school Social Studies?
>
> —Jennifer Shah, Chicago, IL

Teaching for social justice is an increasing emphasis within many teacher education programs, including our own. At Alison's university, for example, faculty guide candidates in examining justice-oriented approaches to curriculum, pedagogy, and assessment. They model approaches to theorizing with K–12 students about contextually relevant issues of (in)equity and justice, and require candidates to develop standards-aligned curriculum that addresses locally relevant issues of social justice. Her candidates work collaboratively with practicing teachers to examine and enact justice-oriented practices in diverse urban classrooms. Over the last 14 years at three different universities, Nick has encouraged teacher candidates and experienced teachers alike to develop strong, trusting relationships with their students and communities, center their teaching in students' lived experiences, and create engaging and critical curricula using rigorous, student-centered methods like Socratic Seminar historical simulations and experientials, and youth participatory action research, among others. His teacher candidates have completed ethnographic studies of students and neighborhoods, designed action research projects, and participated in community mapping, guided by their own justice-oriented research questions. In the courses Ruchi teaches, she guides teachers to think about how they might translate their visions of social justice into a context where standardization and accountability are often the norm. For example, in her course, "Teaching Social Studies, Literacy, and Social Justice," Ruchi blends theory with practice, discussing ways in which students can teach social studies for social justice while also navigating challenges related to the day-to-day realities of teaching. Students are asked to create social studies units guided by a framework she designed (Agarwal-Rangnath, 2013), which integrate social justice ideals and align with school- and university-requirements related to the Common Core State Standards (CCSS). Justice-oriented teacher educators across the country describe similar practices within their own classrooms and communities (e.g., Miller, 2010).

While assignments like these emerge from our commitment to social justice education, they also reflect our experience as K–12 teachers who had to navigate the myriad of demands associated with teaching in accountability-driven schools. Collectively, we have spent 45 years teaching and supporting teachers in diverse urban and suburban classrooms. We know how challenging it can be to teach to one's conscience in contemporary classrooms, and strive to prepare our candidates to enact justice from Day 1 in the classroom.

However, research suggests that even those teachers with strong social justice orientations struggle to build, integrate, and enact social justice pedagogies in their first classrooms (Agarwal, 2011; Agarwal, Epstein, Oppenheim, Oyler, & Sonu, 2010; Cochran-Smith et al., 2009; Dover, 2013a, 2013b; Gorski, 2010; Henning, 2013; Picower, 2011). Emphases on high-stakes testing and accountability often conflict with teachers' social justice leanings, and require teachers to negotiate what and how they want to teach within the context of their individual school settings. With standards-based movements in place and gaining more momentum each year, new teachers face increased pressure to figure out what and how to teach given new academic benchmarks. For many history/social studies teachers, who already face pressure to teach an increasingly comprehensive curriculum while preparing students for standardized tests, this also means finding ways to incorporate the CCSS literacy standards into their existing curriculum and instruction. We see this as both an opportunity and challenge, especially for teachers with a commitment to promoting critical literacy and social justice within the high-stakes context associated with the CCSS.

ABOUT THIS BOOK

This project emerged out of Ruchi's (Agarwal-Rangnath, 2013) examination of justice-oriented approaches to teaching social studies in the elementary grades, and all three authors' desire to highlight the vision, voice, and experience of teachers who use their agency to enact justice within and despite accountability-driven classrooms. Our initial call for contributions invited veteran secondary social studies teachers to share "letters to new teachers" that offered advice for grappling with, building, and implementing justice-oriented curriculum in the age of the CCSS. We were curious: How are justice-oriented social studies teachers responding to changing mandates?

We publicized this project within an array of justice-oriented and social studies-related networks and organizations, distributing our call to teachers in our personal address books and posting it on public listservs and websites. Ultimately, 20 teachers submitted letters for this project; these teachers are described in Appendix A, and their letters are published in full on our website at www.socialstudiesforsocialjustice.com.

Some of the teachers in this book were our own students, and entered their first classroom in the years leading up to the CCSS; others have 20 or more years of experience navigating multiple sets of content standards, state and federal regulations, and shifts in educational priorities. The teachers in this book are ethnically, geographically, and experientially diverse, with between 3 and 20 years of experience teaching social studies in urban and suburban schools across 11 states. They include 13 women and 7 men, and 7 teachers who identify as people of color; 14 teachers identified as White or European American, 3 as Latino/a, 1 as Indian, 3 as Asian, and 1 as Sinhalese (Southeast Asian). Collectively, these teachers have taught social studies in secondary classrooms throughout the country, with different state content standards and curricular emphases. Some of the teachers work in public schools that share their commitment to social justice; others in charter school networks that have faced criticism for their ties to corporate education reform. Eight of the teachers in this book are also teacher educators; three are currently enrolled in doctoral programs. All of the teachers are united by their commitment to academically rigorous, justice-oriented social studies practice, and their desire to share their vision, curriculum, and advice with new teachers preparing to enter the classroom. Although our study draws from the voices and experiences of secondary social studies teachers, we believe that the themes, lessons, and tokens of advice presented in our book will be helpful to justice-oriented teachers across all grade levels.

TEACHING FOR SOCIAL JUSTICE IN THE AGE OF STANDARDS

There are many approaches to teaching for social justice, and published accounts cite a wide range of conceptual frameworks, including democratic education, critical pedagogy, culturally responsive education, ethnic studies, multicultural education, and social justice education (see Agarwal-Rangnath, 2013; Cochran-Smith, 2010; Dover, 2009, 2013b; Gorski, 2010; Grant & Agosto, 2008; Hytten & Bettez, 2011; North, 2006, 2008; Sleeter & Grant, 2007; Tintiangco-Cubales et al., 2015; Young, 2006). Contemporary interpretations of teaching for social justice emerged from this broad foundation and reflect the imperative to enact justice within the context of increasing emphasis on standards-based and accountability-driven schooling.

Teachers' social justice visions manifest in a wide range of curricular and pedagogical emphases, including a commitment to learning about the lives of students and their communities (Ladson-Billings, 1995; Sleeter, 2011) and developing academically rigorous curriculum that supports the learning and achievement of all students in the classroom (Cochran-Smith, 2004; Dover, 2013a, 2013b; Haberman, 1995; Ladson-Billings, 1994; Sleeter, 2005; Zeichner, 2003). Justice-oriented teachers see themselves as both responsible for and capable of challenging and altering an educational system that is not adequately serving large numbers of children, particularly poor children, children of color, and children with special needs (Oakes & Lipton, 2003; Zollers, Albert, & Cochran-Smith, 2000), and encourage their students to join them in examining and making change in their schools, communities, and the world (Dover, 2016; Nieto, 2000; Oakes & Lipton, 2003). Finally, justice-oriented teachers engage in educational activism as they work in and around policy constraints to reform and restructure curriculum (Bigelow, Harvey, Karp, & Miller, 2001; Horn, 2003; Sambell & McDowell, 1998).

In social studies classrooms, justice-oriented teachers use curriculum and pedagogies intended to foster students' critical examination of past and present histories, analysis of multiple historical and contemporary perspectives, and ability to imagine possibilities of social change in their world today. Justice-oriented social studies teachers explicitly acknowledge that history includes a number of movements, changes, and contributions that are the result of the efforts of women, people of color, youth, and other traditionally excluded groups (Bigelow & Peterson, 1998; Tintiangco-Cubales et al., 2015). They interrogate and examine the texts used in social studies classrooms and address examples of bias that "den[y] students the opportunity to benefit from the knowledge, perspectives, and understanding to be gained from studying other cultural groups' experiences and attaining the intercultural competency to work with everyone" (Johnson, 2007, p. 146). In sum, social justice-oriented social studies teachers work intentionally to challenge normative thought by integrating multiple perspectives into the curriculum, especially the voices of those dominated, marginalized, or traditionally excluded in texts. They connect the stories of struggle and resistance to contemporary social justice issues and make connections between historical events and present-day circumstances. In addition, teachers and students work collaboratively to make change in their school and community.

THE HISTORY OF SOCIAL STUDIES STANDARDS

Many of the justice-oriented philosophical and pedagogical approaches mentioned above conflict in form and purpose with accountability-driven education policy; a movement sparked in 1983 with the publication of *A Nation at Risk* (National Commission on Excellence, 1983) and institutionalized by the No Child Left Behind Act of 2001. These policies rely on students' standardized test performance as the primary measure of student learning, resulting in widespread alignment between disciplinary curriculum and testing requirements. After the passage of No Child Left Behind, and with it a further emphasis placed on the achievement and testing of students solely in the areas of English/language arts and mathematics, social studies teachers were also inclined to focus more of their teaching attention on literacy development, and found themselves even further marginalized as a discipline (Au, 2009, 2013a). In many elementary classrooms, time spent on social studies instruction has been completely eliminated, and in secondary social studies classrooms, instructional time is periodically taken up by test-taking practice.

In addition to pressures associated with standardized testing, justice-oriented social studies teachers are accountable to the organization and emphases of social studies curricular frameworks passed by state legislatures across the country. Since the publication and dissemination of the report of the NEA Committee on the Social Studies in 1916, little has changed in the pattern and order of social studies course offerings in K–12 classrooms (Marker, 2006; Marker & Mehlinger, 1992). State social studies curricular frameworks are generally organized around lists of historical events and figures, and historical, economic, and governmental "facts," with little overall emphasis on social studies concepts, disciplinary skills, or critical thinking. Moreover, efforts have been made by multiple social studies/history organizations to suggest sets of standards/guidelines for social studies curriculum at the nationwide level, with an emphasis on critical thinking, historical analysis, democratic citizenship, and thematic curricular organization (e.g., National Council for the Social Studies, 2010; National Governors Association, 2010). Although state lawmakers usually insist that frameworks like these are not to be used to enforce the enactment of a *type* of teaching, the impact of the accountability movement's strict alignment of these curricular frameworks to state-adopted textbooks and high-stakes standardized tests has resulted in just that: a dominant pattern of social studies instruction characterized by text-oriented, whole-group, teacher-centered approaches aimed toward the transmission of "factual" information (Cuban, 1991; Ross, 2014). For justice-oriented teachers, this has meant learning to "teach against the grain" (Cochran-Smith, 1991) as they develop strategies for promoting justice within and despite hostile political and educational contexts.

STANDARDIZATION AND ACCOUNTABILITY

The CCSS are the product of a public–private partnership designed to ensure students are prepared for the demands of the U.S. workforce (Hagopian, 2014). The standards have been widely criticized for their corporate roots (e.g., Au, 2013b; Leahey, 2013; Schneider, 2015), a critique that we share. Moreover, the English Language Arts and Literacy Standards have been challenged for their overemphasis on the close reading and production of informational text rather than literature and creative writing. For content area teachers, the implementation of the CCSS also brings a dramatic reconceptualization of their role in fostering students' literacy skills: The standards include specific requirements regarding reading and writing in the disciplines. Thus, despite the many risks and limitations inherent in standards-driven reforms, we also see opportunities for justice-oriented social studies teachers to use the adoption of the CCSS to foreground critical literacy and reimagine their approach to teaching important disciplinary concepts.

The authors of the CCSS describe them as a set of flexible guidelines designed to inform instruction, arguing that they "define what all students are expected to know and be able to do, not how teachers should teach" (National Governors Association, 2010, p. 6). They claim that they are not seeking to define curriculum, noting that "while the standards make references to some particular forms of content, including mythology, foundational U.S. documents, and Shakespeare, they do not—indeed cannot—enumerate all or even most of the content that students should learn. The standards must therefore be complemented by a well-developed, content-rich curriculum" (p. 6). However, as states seek to ensure their students are meeting the new standards, many are turning toward packaged curricular materials marketed as aligned to the demands of the Common Core (Brooks & Dietz, 2012/13). We see this as a deeply troubling corollary impact of the CCSS. When schools and states implement the CCSS by purchasing materials created and marketed by external corporate entities, they limit teachers' ability to engage in the justice-oriented, localized curricular innovations described in this book.

Moreover, as with any standard-based reform initiative, teachers are increasingly required to focus their classroom instruction and assessments on the priorities of the new standards. High-stakes standardized assessments, like Partnership for Assessment of Readiness for College and Careers (PARCC) tests, have been implemented to evaluate students' mastery of the content. In many cases, the results of these tests are tied to teacher-, school-, and district-level policies that carry financial rewards and punishments related to students' test scores. This creates a high-stakes environment that puts immense pressure on teachers and students to avoid being labeled as "failing" under the new educational model, one which encourages districts to devote less time to less-frequently tested disciplines like social studies (Au, 2013a). With the new assessments in place, teachers are faced with the challenge to teach not only what they consider necessary for their students' learning overall, but also the specific skills and content required to perform well on the standardized tests.

Given the focus on literacy and mathematics, social studies teachers may find themselves concentrating more on teaching students literacy skills that will be tested on the assessments versus critical social studies content. In this respect, how the standards are tested and the accountability measures attached to the standards may work to define teachers' curricular decisions. Even as teachers may see flexibility and creativity with the new standards, how students are tested and what is on the tests may force teachers to negotiate what and how they want to teach (Au, 2009, 2013a; Ross, Mathison, & Vinson, 2014). Ayers (2001) argues that high-stakes tests "constrain teachers' energies and minds, dictating a disastrously narrow range of activities and experiences" (p. 114). As new teachers feel compelled to restructure their curricular goals in order to cover content that will be on the tests (Au, 2009, 2013a; Ayers, 2001; Ross, Mathison, & Vinson, 2014), it is imperative that justice-oriented teachers find ways to uphold their commitment to teach for social justice so that they may engage students in an understanding of history that is critical, complex, and inclusive of voices that are often marginalized or silenced in our mainstream texts.

JUSTICE-ORIENTED RESPONSES TO THE COMMON CORE STANDARDS

For social studies teachers, the CCSS create both the opportunity and imperative to foreground critical literacy and disciplinary thinking alongside specific social studies content. Some of the teachers in this book welcome aspects of this curricular shift, focusing on the ways CCSS is inherently aligned with their approach to student-centered, justice-oriented curriculum and pedagogy. When teachers draw from this stance, which we describe as *embracing* the standards, they see the adoption of the CCSS as offering increased curricular flexibility and as validating their emphasis on teaching traditionally marginalized histories. These teachers see the CCSS not as a shift but as a recognition of the importance of teaching students to think critically about key social studies concepts and skills.

In addition to capitalizing on what they describe as the curricular flexibility and literacy emphases of the CCSS, justice-oriented social studies teachers can also approach the CCSS as an opportunity to redefine social studies curriculum as inherently justice-oriented. Teachers adopting this perspective—which we characterize as *reframing* social studies curriculum in response to the CCSS—see the new standards as an opportunity to subvert dominant curricular and pedagogical paradigms by recentering issues of equity, social location, and justice. For teachers operating from this stance, the shift toward CCSS creates an imperative for justice-oriented social studies teachers to take up the National Governors Association's invitation to "teachers, curriculum developers, and states to determine how these goals should be reached and what additional topics should be addressed" (National Governors Association, 2010, p. 4). Teachers using the standards to reframe curriculum emphasize the importance of collaboratively developing and disseminating justice-oriented social studies curriculum, examples of which are included in the chapters that follow.

However, justice-oriented social studies teachers are also acutely aware of the ways the CCSS are being used to justify top-down curricular mandates and ever-increasing testing requirements. For example, while teachers may appreciate the CCSS's emphasis on critical literacy, they are also acutely aware of the limitations and implications of increasing standardization. They caution against the CCSS's glorification of close reading and resultant decontextualization of historical interpretation. They invite colleagues to question the evolution of the CCSS, asking whom these new standards benefit, and how justice-oriented teachers can avoid inadvertently institutionalizing and reifying corporate education reforms. These teachers highlight the importance of *resisting* the CCSS in order to protect justice-oriented curriculum and pedagogy within standards-driven classrooms, and share their strategies for collective action on behalf of their students and communities.

In the chapters that follow, we will introduce you to the 20 teachers whose voices and experiences inform this volume. In Part I of this book, we examine the multiple ways justice-oriented teachers are strategically responding to the CCSS, using curricular examples of their approach to embracing, reframing, and resisting the standards and their emphases. In Part II, we move from theory to praxis, analyzing justice-oriented teachers' curricular and pedagogical practices. In Chapter 3, we focus on how justice-oriented teachers use the CCSS's emphasis on critical disciplinary literacy as a springboard for comprehensive analyses of key social studies concepts. In Chapter 4, we examine how teachers build, curate, and prioritize content that engages students in justice-oriented analysis of contextually relevant historical and contemporary topics, using examples from teachers' classrooms to illustrate their approach. Chapter 5 explores teachers' use of student-centered, inquiry-driven, and action-oriented pedagogies as they work collaboratively with students to apply their learning within and beyond the classroom. Throughout, we interweave excerpts from teachers' letters with examples of their curriculum, focusing on how they are using the CCSS as an opportunity to enact academically rigorous, justice-oriented social studies practice.

In Part III, we broaden our analysis to examine how teachers develop, support, and sustain their identities as justice-oriented teachers in standards-driven classrooms. Chapter 6 focuses on the practical and philosophical influences that informed teachers' development as justice-oriented teachers. Our discussion examines the role of mentorship, preservice preparation, professional development, activism, and social justice vision as guiding teachers' daily practices. In Chapter 7, we examine some of the challenges faced by justice-oriented teachers, including institutional and resistance, lack of resources, and external pressures toward standardization. We highlight teachers' advice regarding how they overcame these challenges, with a focus on the role of justice-oriented teacher communities and professional networks as a strategy for sustaining and supporting their work. Finally, in Chapter 8, we grapple with the political implications of teaching for social justice, as we examine teachers' efforts to engage, and encourage students to engage, in taking action in the interest of social justice.

CHAPTER 2

Conceptual Approaches to the Common Core

Published accounts of teaching for social justice illustrate the robust diversity in teachers' embodiment of locally relevant, discipline-specific, curriculum and pedagogy (see, e.g., Agarwal-Rangnath, 2013; Bigelow et al., 2001; Dover, 2013a, 2016; Henning, 2013; Sleeter & Grant, 2007; Tintiangco-Cubales et al., 2015). However, there are also common threads woven throughout teachers' practice. In this chapter, we focus on three ways the veteran history/social studies teachers in this volume respond to the CCSS, and its implications for their daily curricular and pedagogical practices. While some teachers could be characterized as primarily working from one of these conceptual frameworks, most shifted strategically among all three stances in response to the unique demands of a given curricular, pedagogical, or political context.

EMBRACING

Despite the many troubling implications of the CCSS, many justice-oriented teachers remained hopeful about elements of the CCSS that they see as aligned with what they were already doing or wanted to do in the classroom. To them, the CCSS offer more flexibility than previous social studies requirements; thus, greater latitude in choosing materials for use in the classroom. Under the CCSS, curriculum has the potential to be more flexible, student-centered, and grounded in critical thinking. Before the CCSS, many teachers felt they were expected to deliver history content as a predetermined set of facts prepackaged for them in textbooks. With the implementation of CCSS, some teachers now believed they would be able to take greater steps to move beyond the master narrative portrayed in textbooks, and teach social studies and history from a perspective that was inclusive of voices that were traditionally marginalized or silenced entirely. Additionally, these teachers hoped that the CCSS gave them the opportunity to incorporate more literacy and language development skills into their curriculum. For teachers working from the stance of *embracing*, the CCSS, and their perceived flexibility, presented an opportunity for them to reclaim their work as justice-oriented social studies educators.

In this section, we use excerpts from the letters of Eran De Silva, Laura Einhorn, Dawn Fontaine, Tom Skjervheim, and Michael Swogger to illustrate the opportunity teachers found in the CCSS. In the excerpts, each social justice educator describes how and why a teacher might embrace the CCSS. They also offer advice and words of wisdom in regards to enacting justice-oriented curriculum that resonates with the emphases of CCSS.

Merging Visions of Social Justice with the CCSS

Eran DeSilva, a director of professional development and social studies teacher in San Jose, California, sees the CCSS as a tool to guide her practice in preparing students to be activists in today's society. As an advocate for justice, she believes the CCSS to not be an obstacle in her teaching, but rather finds the standards to be aligned with the skills she believes are important to instill in her students. Eran asserts that being an activist in today's society requires a specific skill set and these skills are integrated into the CCSS. She explains:

> Any advocate who works for justice must be a strong critical thinker, a thoughtful listener, and an effective communicator. The framework of CCSS outlines standards that will help students to obtain these skills. So when I am creating curriculum and instructing my students about the world around them, I can use CCSS to help guide my practice.

In this excerpt, we can see how Eran is able to integrate the CCSS into her vision of social justice teaching. When creating her curriculum, Eran draws particularly on learning goals that evoke critical thinking, thoughtful listening, and effective communicating. She does not see the CCSS as a roadblock, but rather a guide to help her pursue her passion of teaching for social justice. For example, when teaching the first skill, critical thinking, Eran challenges her students to analyze information and think critically about what they read. The CCSS asks students to "evaluate sources of information" (CCSS.ELA-LITERACY.RH.11-12.3) and "integrate information from diverse sources . . . noting discrepancies among sources" (CCSS.ELA-LITERACY.RH.11-12.9). For Eran, each of these learning goals lend themselves to critical thinking, which she sees as a key aspect of justice-oriented teaching. Eran feels that teaching students to evaluate sources of information is an invaluable skill that will allow them to be critical of myriad issues, such as ballot initiatives, Supreme Court rulings, media and political campaigns, and advertising. Eran further explains: "Students must digest and deconstruct what they are reading rather than passively taking in information" so that they are empowered to analyze what they are "told and sold."

While Eran is able to teach her students about the world around them and think critically about what they see, she is also able to meet the CCSS. Through Eran's analysis of the CCSS, she believes that one can use the CCSS to guide their practice by translating the CCSS into objectives that directly align with her focus on social justice. Because the standards are skill-based, Eran feels she is able to adapt the standards so that they fit with her vision of teaching. In Eran's case the CCSS allows her to create curriculum that is grounded in critical thinking so that she can prepare students to be activists within their school and community. In her letter, Eran explains that she values social justice and her students' potential to be agents of change. She asserts that she will use the tools given to her, including the CCSS, to empower her students to "create a more inclusive and just community." For Eran, the CCSS is an avenue, not a roadblock, to achieving her goals. She is able to reclaim her work as a social justice educator and carry on with her passion to teach for social justice.

Laura Einhorn, a 9th-grade history teacher in San Lorenzo, CA, finds the shift to the CCSS to be "an opportunity to imagine creative and critical courses." To her, the CCSS represents an opportunity to imagine creative and critical courses with more spaces to teach for social justice. For example, "Determine the central ideas or information of a primary or secondary source" (CCSS.ELA-LITERACY.RH.11-12.2) affords much more flexibility than previous state standards such "Describe the emergence of Romanticism in art and literature (e.g., the poetry of William Blake and William Wordsworth), social criticism (e.g., the novels of Charles Dickens), and the move away from Classicism in

Europe" (California History Content Standard 10.3.7). Laura describes her 12th-grade course on race, class, gender, and sexuality as the product of this curricular flexibility:

> I'm taking advantage of this leeway afforded by the move to CCSS to write a new course on race, class, gender, and sexuality. In this seminar course for high school seniors, we will practice all of the foundational literacy skills demanded by the CCSS.

Through this excerpt we can see that the CCSS does not derail Laura from her vision to teach for social justice. Rather, from Laura's perspective, the focus on pedagogy and skills in the CCSS opens "a window of opportunity for history teachers to regain control over the content of our courses." She details how she meets the standards and maintains her vision of social justice in this excerpt:

> Instead of "evaluating authors' different points of view on the same historical event or issue" in the context of the Federalist papers or Adam Smith's *Wealth of Nations*, we will hold up Ta-Nehisi Coates, "The Case for Reparations" against Kevin Williamson's response in the *National Review*. Our texts within the "11-CCR text complexity band" will be written by Gloria Anzaldua, Barbara Ehrenrich, Michelle Alexander, and bell hooks. Using these relevant and timely texts, students will write weekly literature reviews using the "They Say/I Say" structure in order to "evaluate an author's premises, claims, and evidence by corroborating or challenging them with other information." They will prepare and moderate class discussions. I am confident that the rigorous discourse, reading, and writing in this classroom will more than satisfy the baseline established by the CCSS test; but the content will enable all of us to explore our own identities and gain a more complete understanding of the historical underpinnings of the structural inequities of our society today.

In this newly created course, Laura is able to meet standards, but with texts that challenge students to look at history from a critical lens. She leans on the learning goal of "evaluating authors," to present her students with texts that challenge them to think critically about their own identities and the structural inequities of our society. Laura also uses the flexibility of the CCSS to enact student-driven research projects. She believes that through these projects she can reinforce key literacy skills, prepare students for college, and give students control over their education. She leans on Cammarota and Fine's (2008) *Revolutionizing Education: Youth Participatory Action Research in Motion* to design student-driven and rigorous research projects. Laura provides the templates, deadlines, and instruction on research methods and writing for the project, but requires the idea and impetus for the project to come from her students. With the move to the CCSS, Laura is able to imagine and create a critical course. She embraces the ways the new standards allow her to hold true to her vision of social justice teaching, while still teaching the foundational literacy skills her students need.

Dawn Fontaine is a 9th-grade world history teacher who enacts her vision of social justice through the integration of Freirean critical literacy (Freire, 1970, 1974). Dawn believes that students should learn that, "they have the right and responsibility to ask questions." Dawn asks students to explore why the voices or experiences of certain people or groups are missing from texts. She also invites students to think about how their interpretation of a historical event might be different if the text were written from another point of view. She believes history should be taught through the exploration of multiple perspectives as she states, "educating students about history is about showing students how to identify perspective, then they determine what they think about it." In her mind, "every historical event, speech and act is interpreted in multiple ways through multiple perspectives. One's perspective is influenced by their life's experiences." For Dawn, teaching students about history is directly linked to teaching students about multiple perspectives and the bias in historical interpretations.

Dawn sees the CCSS as an opportunity to teach her students "skills that open access to the language and culture of power" (Delpit, 1988). She shares, "teaching students skills that are transferrable across context and will allow them to access and navigate the dominant culture is an act of social justice and one that positions me as an ally with my students." Dawn explains that reading, writing, speaking, and listening as literacy skills are the skills valued in the culture of power and are prioritized by the CCSS. For this reason, she believes that teaching students the CCSS is preparing her students to access and participate in a culture of power. In this sense, teaching the CCSS is not removed or isolated from Dawn's beliefs as a social justice educator; rather, Dawn's view of the standards offers her greater possibility as she is able to merge her vision for social justice with the objectives and skills purported by the CCSS.

Advice for Embracing the CCSS

Like many of the other teachers presented in this chapter, Tom Skjervheim, now a senior program associate at ConnectEd (The California Center for College and Career), believes the CCSS not only aligns with but also supports his vision of social justice teaching. He suggests that, "teaching to the CCSS well is social justice education. In the face of overwhelming systemic inequities, teaching all students to be masterful critical thinkers, problem solvers, and communicators is one of the most important responsibilities of a social justice educator." Tom believes that teaching the types of skills included in the CCSS is a necessary component of being a justice-oriented educator. For this reason, Tom advises novice teachers to "become great at teaching the CCSS." He argues, "whether we like it or not, we are (or soon will be) accountable to CCSS assessments like Smarter Balanced. . . . As we individually and collectively improve our pedagogy to better reflect the skills and competencies of the CCSS, we are also building our strategic capacity to weather the next storm of reaction to educational policy." In other words, Tom believes that as educators work to align their work with the current pressures of CCSS, they concurrently work to becoming skilled at navigating educational policy. From Tom's perspective, teachers can teach the standards and also maintain their commitment to teach for social justice.

Michael Swogger, an adjunct professor of education at Penn State Harrisburg insists that teachers not worry about the CCSS and offers the following advice:

> The *CCSS*, with its focus on the language arts, encourages social studies teachers to do their part by helping enhance students' reading and writing abilities, to better develop their analytical skills, and to practice deeper critical thinking.

In this excerpt, Michael explains how the CCSS can support one's vision of social justice teaching. Michael claims that the CCSS can help to enrich our teaching through a focus on language arts. Under CCSS, social studies teachers can focus more on challenging our students to be better readers and writers, while also developing students' analytical and critical thinking skills.

In sum, each of the teachers' presented in this section embrace the possibilities of the CCSS to support their visions of social justice teaching. Eran described how she uses the CCSS to guide her teaching, while Laura used the shift to CCSS to write a course on race, class, gender, and sexuality. Dawn focused on the CCSS's emphasis on critical literacy and multiple perspectives, while Tom saw his commitment to high expectations reflected in the skills and competencies of the CCSS. Finally, Michael explained how the CCSS, with its focus on literacy, can enrich our social studies teaching. By embracing elements of the CCSS that align with their own visions, each of these teachers were able to use the shift to CCSS to further their efforts toward justice.

REFRAMING

While some teachers embraced the ways the CCSS aligned with or reinforced their approach to teaching social studies, others focused on the opportunity to (re)define or *reframe* curriculum under the CCSS. For these teachers, the CCSS offer an opportunity to subvert dominant curricular and pedagogical paradigms by recentering issues of equity, social location, and justice.

Redefining Social Studies Curriculum under the CCSS

Brian Gibbs, a former teacher with 16 years of experience teaching history and American government in East Los Angeles, encourages new teachers to take an active role in defining justice-oriented teaching under the CCSS.

> What CCSS and teaching will become is going to be decided largely by you, your choices, your movements, your creativity, your associations, and your ability to avoid or reframe and outright refuse. Revolutionaries exist amongst us. They have and always will. Complete system change, throwing off the old and building something wholly new, is incredibly complex and difficult. Though revolutionaries are needed, they are rare. Freedom Schools, Central Park East Elementary and Secondary Schools, Urban Academy in New York City, the New York Standards Performance Consortium (NYSPC), and the Scrap the MAP Campaign have all taken revolutionary steps to tear down, re-imagine and rebuild. However, these revolutionaries stand on the shoulders of the renegades—the ones who stay in the more traditional setting but don't teach like it and with students labeled as failures but don't treat them as such. Renegades are like the outlaws Tom Robbins defines, "Unwilling to wait for

> mankind to improve, the outlaw lives as if that day were here. Outlaws are can openers in the supermarket of life." May this be you.

Brian goes on to describe teachers who use standards-aligned curriculum to enact justice as "warriors" whose daily instructional decisions and collegial participation can shape the future of teaching and learning. "Rather than the shout on the street or the angry frustrated denouncements of the department or faculty meeting, it is the whispered conversation in the hallway, the lunch time spent talking and planning, the lesson or unit shared that makes the most difference." Brian describes his experiences working with colleagues to ensure their curriculum was thematically aligned, grounded in critical pedagogy, and included all of the required social studies skills and content. Ultimately, this led to changes in the instructional requirements at his school, as he and his colleagues convinced their principal and superintendent of the importance and validity of their approach to teaching social studies.

Brian's emphasis of the critical role of teachers in redefining curriculum echoes the Design Considerations of the CCSS themselves, which note the opportunity for "teachers, curriculum developers, and states to determine how these goals should be reached and what additional topics should be addressed" (National Governors Association, 2010, p. 4). However, in practice, the CCSS are often used to justify top-down, standardized curriculum.

Like many, Michael Swogger, a teacher introduced in the previous section, wrestled with the contradictions inherent in doing justice-oriented work in standards-driven contexts. While he embraced some aspects of the CCSS (see above), he is also concerned about the ways they are frequently used to limit teachers' curricular and pedagogical autonomy.

> You will be watched much more closely, ensuring that nearly everything you teach conforms to stricter, top-down mandated lesson planning and assessment strategies—all aligned with state and national standards. Your performance will be measured, and the quality of your teaching judged, at least in part by your and your school's student performance on *CCSS* aligned state exams. There is little chance that any issues of social justice, and your ability to arouse your students' enthusiasm and passions for them, will be assessed as part of how educated your students are becoming.

However, Michael, like many teachers profiled in this book, chooses to use this increased emphasis on alignment as an opportunity for teacher-activists to redefine social studies curriculum, asking:

> Is there any way to teach social justice by any means other than what *CCSS* so brazenly advances as novel? *CCSS* is not going to stop *you* from promoting a strong, democratic classroom dialogue on issues of race, sex and gender, and class. The standards are not going to prevent *you* from engaging your students in problem- and inquiry-based learning projects on the fundamental nature of poverty or institutionalized discrimination. Even when you feel hamstrung by the emphasis on standards-driven instruction and high-stakes exams, you can move confidently forward knowing that your dedication to social justice will both outweigh and outlive the skills and content the *CCSS* purport to advance.

Despite Michael's belief that social studies teachers can use the CCSS to enact justice-centered teaching, he also recognizes the challenges inherent in that work: "I will not lie and say that teaching in the *CCSS* era will be easy. Teaching itself is one of the most difficult jobs there is, and the *CCSS* are not making it any better." However, by using CCSS as a jumping-off point, Michael is able to provoke his students' examination of complex social justice topics, asking them to analyze the contemporary relevance of rights and freedoms in Colonial America ("Does the Tea Party represent a revival of America's revolutionary ideals") or create evidence-based analyses of pressing political issues ("Should America adopt public financing of political campaigns? Does Affirmative Action advance racial equality? Do we need national health insurance?") By centralizing issues of social justice within a comprehensive and rigorous social studies curriculum, Michael redefines social studies education as an inherently critical and transformative process.

However, Michael's approach also highlights a significant challenge associated with teaching for social justice in standards-driven classrooms: the necessity that teachers have both a comprehensive foundation in their disciplines and a willingness to engage in the difficult work of curricular authorship and activism. Jared Kushida, a teacher at a Knowledge Is Power Program (KIPP) charter high school in San Lorenzo, California, articulates this tension:

> Oh, how easy and nice it would be to just take that teacher Blue Pill and assign readings from old textbooks, use corporate curriculum made by companies who sell their workbooks at

> seminars in hotels near the airport, and of course, how easy it would be to just teach to standardized tests. . . .[However, writing original curriculum] is especially important in the era of CCSS, which will present for-profit curriculum companies a golden opportunity to strike it rich by convincing schools and districts to buy their materials. We know these materials will not do anything to engage our students in meaningful work, so we need to work hard at designing curriculum for them that is both transformative and rigorous. In the long run, testing regimes, standardization trends, accountability movements, and education "reform" will come and go, but great teaching will outlive them all. Just remember, in education it is people who matter, not things.

For Jared, like many of the teachers profiled in this book, the emphases of the CCSS both invite and require teachers to redefine social studies curriculum as student-driven and justice-centered.

In order to meet the challenges associated with teaching for social justice in an increasingly accountability-driven context, effective justice-oriented teachers have a comprehensive foundation in their content area, fluency in state and national mandates, and the personal and practical resources necessary to supplement materials supplied by their schools and districts. Rory Tannenbaum, a middle school social studies teacher from South Carolina, argues that:

> With CCSS permeating so much of the educational landscape, it is essential that we find associations between critical themes in social studies education and the content and performance-based standards students must master. To that end, educators must seek to understand how the CCSS (as well as similar and corresponding initiatives) can encompass theories and principles of social justice within the classroom.

Rory offers the example of how teachers can use the CCSS's emphasis on speaking and listening to center critical discourse in social studies classrooms, noting that "as students progress throughout their K–12 education, this expectation is made more complex and age-appropriate." While Rory notes that "the CCSS never explicitly say the purpose of developing students capable of participating in discussions as being related to social justice, educators at any level should understand how an association between the two could be made." For Rory, the CCSS offers an opportunity to reframe justice-oriented pedagogy as standards-aligned practice.

Reclaiming Professional Expertise

Melissa Gibson, an 8th-grade teacher with experience teaching in Guadalajara, Mexico, Chicago, Los Angeles, and Wisconsin, echoes this theme. She argues that teachers can and should interpret increased emphases on curricular standards as an opportunity for justice-centered transformation.

> Call me crazy, but working within (sometimes hostile) parameters like CCSS has actually made my teaching more robustly justice-oriented. Beginning again in Mexico, I kept remembering a Chicago workshop with a creativity expert. Standards and assessments had us in a chokehold. How could we teach in their grip? This improv coach challenged us: "Creativity is not only dreaming up whatever you want! It is taking what you're given and imaginatively reinventing it. Creativity within structure—it's the improv principle of 'Yes, and. . . .'" Teaching for social justice, particularly in our standardized era, requires creativity. Yes, and: We can take structures like CCSS and do the critical work of teaching for social justice within them.
>
> This should be reassuring: To teach for social justice, you don't have to build curriculum from scratch. But whatever you teach, you must do so critically. Our world—with its myriad injustices, with tangled and misrepresented histories, with social science built on colonizing methodologies—requires critically conscious citizens. After all, this is the work of the critical social sciences: Teaching our students to question the narratives they are fed and to ask questions that can reimagine our world. As Howard Zinn (2002) said, "You can't be neutral on a moving train." Whatever you teach, it's a moving train. What direction are you headed?

For teachers like Melissa, the widespread implementation of the CCSS offers an opportunity to redefine social studies curriculum as both student-driven and justice-centered. When building curriculum, Melissa uses key questions about ownership and perspective to hold herself accountable as a critical educator, asking "Whose voice is missing? . . . How would this (hi)story be different if told from another perspective? How does this connect to the world today?" She then uses the tools and emphases of the CCSS to build alternate curriculum that culminates in a comprehensive "Social Issues Research and Action Project." In the following excerpt, Melissa articulates the relationship between her 8th-graders' investigation into the validity of the Columbus Day holiday and the emphases of the CCSS:

> This is an area where the [CCSS for social studies]—where content takes a backseat to literacy skills—support our work. *Understanding and evaluating texts?* What we practiced in our critical comparison of global news sources. *Analyzing how and from what perspective a text presents information?* The heart of what we learned about bias, perspective, and the single story. *Analyzing different types of sources (facts/opinions, primary/secondary)?* Our investigation of Columbus. *Analyzing and using evidence?* Our editorials and our social issue project. The very thinking and writing skills at the heart of critical social studies are codified by CCSS.

Through an emphasis on student-driven, justice-oriented curriculum, Melissa effectively uses the standards to cast into relief the types of curricular hegemony that dominate public education. Carolina Valdez, an elementary teacher in the Los Angeles Unified School District, employs similar strategies in her approach to "decolonial pedagogy" that interrogates traditional perspectives in social studies classrooms. She argues that:

> Although limitations will always exist within the colonial schooling structures (not much can be done with the grueling month long testing schedule for CCSS), there are always possibilities within the curriculum. This may range from simply tweaking what the current curriculum offers; to building supplemental lessons to ensure your students are receiving a relevant and critical curriculum that meets their needs.

Carolina offers multiple examples of her approach to justice-oriented curricular redefinition under the auspices of the CCSS. When teaching indigenous history, for example, she uses the required textbook as a springboard for an interdisciplinary, justice-centered unit.

> Within my fifth grade social studies textbook, indigenous history was allotted nine pages. Not satisfied with this, I extended the unit for a month, adding supplemental readings from *A Young People's History of the United States* by Howard Zinn, student research projects and models on Native tribes, and built the unit across the subject matter to include CCSS ELA writing standards,

> art, and gender studies. I also included a group investigation of several indigenous peoples across Latin America in the attempt to help my students understand that Native Americans are not confined to the U.S. borders, and that Latinos are themselves indigenous.

Carolina's commitment to centering nondominant narratives is an act of both curricular and political activism. In describing her approach to teaching ethnic studies, Carolina notes that:

> Understanding the role Ethnic Studies courses in college played in my identity development and political consciousness, I felt it unethical to wait in hopes that my students make it through the pipeline to college in order to receive such content. Thus, looking for overlap with CCSS ELA standards, I developed a research project in which my fifth graders studied various Freedom Fighters, from Geronimo to Assata Shakur, and supported my students in the creation of the project output of their choosing.

Carolina is using the CCSS to frame a social studies curriculum that is both student-driven and justice-centered. Like all of the teachers profiled throughout this section, Carolina's approach relies on her comprehensive understanding of social studies content, fluency in the demands of the CCSS at her grade level, and ability to critically and creatively reframe the social studies curriculum. Collectively, these teachers' efforts underscore the potential for social studies teachers to redefine a justice-centered social studies education in the CCSS era.

However, despite the strategies articulated by these teachers, not all justice-oriented teachers interpret the shift to the CCSS as a positive change. In the following section, we explore how—and why—justice-oriented teachers are *resisting* the CCSS in their classrooms and communities.

RESISTING

To be a resister—"warrior," "revolutionary," "renegade," and "outlaw," were some of the resistant titles and metaphors offered to new teachers by our veteran letter writers—was a role clearly valued by many of the teachers. Despite the many new possibilities and familiar curricular emphases cited by the teachers in their discussion of either to embrace or reframe the CCSS for justice-oriented social studies teachers' use, a number of teachers also emphasized the need to *resist* this "new" curricular shift.

For some, although the standards may change, the unjust high-stakes accountability policies and testing attached to these standards remain. For others, it is necessary to understand who benefits—and has already benefited—the most from the implementation of CCSS to truly understand why it happened in the first place (see Karp, 2013). And, just as other reforms have come and gone, so will CCSS, but the important work of teaching young people still remains, and teachers will have to choose to resist (or not) those pieces of CCSS that do not serve their students well. Last, there are important social studies-related skills that are missing from the CCSS, which would serve to decontextualize and depersonalize the study of history and human beings. In these ways, the resistance suggested by the teachers is one of deeply understanding the broader historical context of educational reform, the powerful influence of politicians, the wealthy, and large corporations in CCSS's creation and implementation, what may be missing from them, and then acting on that knowledge through various forms of resistance. In Chapter 8, various possible forms of resistance are explained in detail.

To be clear, there is a large amount of risk associated with the resistance suggested by some of our veteran teachers. In transforming curricula in history and social studies, in speaking out against injustices, teachers rewrite "common sense" notions, ideologies, and narratives that have upheld an unjust status quo. Recent dismissals of teachers like Marylin Zuniga, a New Jersey elementary school teacher who asked that her students write get well letters to the hospitalized political prisoner Mumia Abu-Jamal, or Karen Salazar, a Los Angeles social studies teacher who was fired because she was "presenting a biased view of the curriculum" and "indoctrinating her students with Afrocentrism" after including board-approved texts like the writings of Malcolm X and Langston Hughes, show us the risks inherent in making curriculum relevant to our students and standing in solidarity with them.

Who Benefits from the CCSS?

As Tom Skjervheim reminds us in his letter, many of his fellow educators' careers have never known anything other than a standards-driven, high-stakes testing, accountability policy context, and there is no indication that this context will change with the CCSS:

> Law makers, leaders, and teachers have been immersed in a culture of high-stakes testing and accountability. Few teachers

> I work with remember anything other than education driven by multiple choice tests, pacing guides, and district mandates. Even fewer have trust in the people (from local to national) making decisions about what is best for our students. We should embrace standards that emphasize higher-order thinking and communication skills, but we must also learn from our recent mistakes to build strategic systems and programs around the implementation of these standards.

The impact of this high-stakes culture and educational policy on teachers and their students during this era have been devastating. David Jauregui, a 10-year veteran of middle school and high school, has begun to seriously question his choice of career, despite his dedication to his students:

> Maybe I'm finally succumbing to all the pressure from all the teacher scapegoating in the media that turns my stomach. Arne Duncan's CCSS, Vergara v. California [a recent anti-teacher tenure decision], corporatization of education, the emphasis on gadgets over substance, cronyism . . . all these things keep me up at night. Moreover, so many good people are leaving the classroom, for various reasons, moving on to more pay, less stress and better work conditions, and I'm starting to wonder why I don't do the same.

As she sees her role as a critical history teacher, Laura Einhorn believes we must ask some questions of the CCSS and its "new testing regime":

> Who's making money off of these tests? What about the schools with inadequate computers or internet connection? Will test questions with proven bias be thrown out? Wasn't the field test [of Smarter Balanced] a nightmare? Will teachers be forced to "teach to this test" with the same gusto as the [previous] state content standards, robbing teachers of their creativity and local control?

Despite his ability to recognize the opportunity for justice-oriented teachers to use the CCSS effectively, Michael Swogger ultimately echoes Laura and David's skepticism and critique. He notes that business leaders and politicians put the CCSS together hastily with significant financial support from Bill Gates and related industries, and little input from teachers. Also, despite a lack of field testing of the standards, they were enthusiastically embraced by President Obama and Secretary of Education Arne Duncan. As Michael puts it:

> [The CCSS] are a one-size-fits-all pseudo-solution to what ails many of our public schools. The testing industry, which helped to write these standards, is already taking advantage of the vast new markets the standards created (see Figueroa, 2013; Ravitch, 2013). In the end, the [CCSS] is part of a thinly veiled effort to reform public education in order to destroy public education, one "failing" school at a time.

Encouragingly, instead of viewing the hasty and well-funded efforts of the CCSS as something that should cause despair in new teachers, Michael views it as something that has happily already incited resistance, from both sides of the political spectrum, and within schools:

> Students and teachers across the nation are standing up to the high-stakes testing requirements that the [CCSS] has helped to intensify (see Johnson, 2013). More parents are opting their children out of statewide exams (see Brown, 2014). Some states have even begun to drop the [CCSS] altogether (see Ujifusa, 2014). From a macro level, one can see the pushback bearing fruit. And as a social studies teacher, I am sure you can easily see what the protests are about: fairness, equity, and treating our children with respect. In other words, social justice.

The Need for Social Justice Remains

Much of the present resistance to the CCSS mirrors resistance directed at other local state, and federal "reform" policy efforts of the past. In order to keep their focus on serving their students well, a number of teachers offer the advice of "rid[ing] the waves of educational policies that come and go over time" and/or "navigat[ing] the revolving door of educational mandates," as Isabel Morales, a founding social studies teacher at Los Angeles High School of the Arts puts it. Prentice Chandler, a former social studies teacher in rural Alabama who is now a university-based teacher educator, also finds it helpful to see educational mandates as temporary. In his letter, he cites Evans (2006) as reminding teachers that "If you don't like the current direction of curricular reform, take heart, it may not last" (p. 317). So, regardless of these temporary mandates, the imperative in Isabel's classroom of "building an academically empowered community of socially responsible and civically engaged youth," of "teaching for social justice" in all of our teachers' classrooms, and the need for social justice in general, still remains. These mandates should not, and cannot, dictate teaching practice if they are found by teachers to be in conflict with these imperatives. So, according to Prentice:

> You have several pedagogical decisions to make. They can be summarized in a question that one of my methods students asked me, "Can you really teach like this? Should we just play by the rules and then teach this way when we get tenure?" In this question we can see the tension between teaching for social justice and teaching as an act of self-preservation. In an ideal world, the mandates of the state and the ideals encapsulated in social justice would have a symbiotic, give and take, yin-yang relationship. But, we don't live in an ideal education world. The ideals of teaching for social justice and the ideals behind CCSS are in opposition to one another, giving us the impression that we have to pick a side.

In some cases, as was mentioned in some teacher's call to reframe or reclaim the CCSS to serve teaching for social justice, what CCSS advances as "novel" or "new" has been used by teachers for many decades to serve social justice goals. Promoting strong democratic classroom dialogue, engaging students in problem- and inquiry-based learning projects, and developing the skills of critical literacy have always occurred. As Michael emphasized earlier in this chapter, what may sustain teachers the most will be a consistent focus on the transformative impact they have had and will have on their students.

Historians Don't Decontextualize

Lastly, in analyzing what they might continue to do, or refuse to do in their classroom, teachers should also examine what may be missing from the CCSS. As it promotes literacy across the disciplines, it may also be ignoring key discipline-specific social studies literacy skills. According to both Isabel and Lindsey Oakes, a middle school social studies teacher in New York City, there is a strong tendency in the CCSS to emphasize the building of literacy skills that serve to not only decontextualize the application of the skills themselves, but also the content they examine.

For the social studies classroom, although the CCSS gladly move classroom instructional strategies away from traditional, lecture-based, direct instruction toward an emphasis on the reading and analysis of primary sources, and the skill of written argumentation, it "limits student engagement with disciplinary historical approaches to more 'school-like' approaches," according to Lindsey. While some of the reading standards like "cite specific textual evidence to support analysis of primary and secondary sources" (CCSS.ELA-LITERACY.RH.6-8.1) reinforce some of the skills of *close reading* and *corroboration* required to analyze the relationship between a primary source document and a secondary source document (Wineburg, Martin, & Monte-Sano, 2011), there are none that correlate to sourcing or contextualizing. Without these skills, Lindsey tells our teachers, students are likely to take the content of documents at face value, and treat all sources equally as historical evidence. This is antithetical to how historians approach historical evidence.

Even further, CCSS.ELA-LITERACY.RH.6-8.2 calls for students to "provide an accurate summary of the source distinct from prior knowledge or opinions"; this is in contrast to the historical thinking work of corroboration (see Wineburg 1991a, 1991b), which requires readers to consider whether the content of a document fits with or contradicts existing knowledge about a topic, and to assess the reliability of the source accordingly. In the end, by seeking to take a source, a story, an image, out of its context, and take away its humanness (see Ferguson, 2013), the CCSS may, for the social studies classroom, deprioritize what historians actually do. Some justice-oriented teachers fear that by decontextualizing historical concepts in favor of a narrow focus on close reading, the CCSS may inadvertently discourage historians/young citizens from seeking, weighing, and sharing the truth. As Isabel puts it, if we can't "inspir[e] student[s] to *want* to read, write, and think," then we will not have successfully educated students toward becoming "compassionate and resourceful agents of social change."

CONCLUSION

Despite the many ways these justice-oriented teachers vary in their relative emphasis on embracing, critiquing, and resisting the impact of CCSS, they all emphasize the importance of teachers' ability, and right, to think and act for themselves. As Jennifer Shah, a former middle school teacher from Chicago, argues:

> With top down mandates such as the CCSS, educators often forget that they are professionals and not technicians. Reading the introduction to the CCSS carefully one finds that it leaves wiggle room for teachers to decide how to apply the standards, but do not take my word for it. Read the standards yourself, learn about the history of the standards, apply a critical lens such as questioning who benefits from the CCSS.

In addition to this belief, there is also an abiding faith that whatever the CCSS and affiliated mandates throw at them, they will survive it. Michael sums up the perspective of many justice-oriented teachers, encouraging new teachers to embrace the challenges of teaching for justice within and despite the current climate by stating, "For educators like you, dedicated to teaching social justice and instilling in your students a sense of moral responsibility and empathy toward one another, the *CCSS* is not and never will be a major obstacle." Whether in support of embracing, reframing, or resisting, the veteran teachers introduced in this chapter are united by their commitment to social justice and by their encouragement of new teachers to create, implement, and enact justice-oriented social studies curriculum in the classroom regardless of what comes their way.

Part II

FROM THEORY TO PRAXIS: CURRICULAR AND PEDAGOGICAL STRATEGIES

In the chapters in this Part, we examine the ways that teachers translate their commitment to social justice into concrete curricular and pedagogical practices within and despite the demands of standards-driven schooling. In Chapter 3, we focus on how justice-oriented teachers can use the CCSS's emphasis on critical disciplinary literacy as a springboard for comprehensive analyses of key social studies concepts. In Chapter 4, we examine how teachers build, curate, and prioritize content that engages students in a justice-oriented analysis of contextually relevant historical and contemporary topics, using examples from teachers' classrooms to illustrate their approach. Chapter 5 explores teachers' use of student-centered, inquiry-driven, and action-oriented pedagogy as they work collaboratively with students to apply their learning within and beyond the classroom. Throughout, we interweave excerpts from teachers' letters with examples of their curriculum, focusing on how they are using the CCSS as an opportunity to enact an academically rigorous, justice-oriented social studies teaching practice.

CHAPTER 3

Focus on Critical Literacy

Oftentimes when students think of social studies, they think of a course that requires them to memorize facts. Teaching students history by rote, as if it were limited to the simple absorption of historical figures, dates, and events, can make students disinterested and detached from social studies content. When social studies is constructed as the memorization of facts that are then regurgitated onto a test, the true essence of what it means to be a historian gets lost. Investigating history, as historians do, involves a far more complex way of learning and understanding. Historians serve as detectives into our past, "searching for evidence among primary sources to a mystery that can never be completely solved." (Wineburg, 2010, p. 2). As Wineburg explains further:

> History is an argument about what facts should or shouldn't mean. Even when historians are able to piece together the basic story of what happened, they rarely agree about what an event means or what caused it. Historians argue about the past's meaning and what it has to tell us in the present. (p. 2)

Teaching students to think historically (Wineburg, 2010) requires us to engage them in the act of learning to think like a historian. Historians ask critical questions, interrogate multiple texts, question what they read, draw on their background knowledge, and draw conclusions based on the evidence they have gathered. How historians interpret a historical event is largely based on the sources they choose to examine. However, each source is necessarily reflective of the perspectives of its authors, and collectively historical texts can amplify some voices while silencing others. As justice-oriented social studies teachers, how can we develop our students' ability to discern and think critically about the content in texts? How do we challenge students to see the silenced voices of those traditionally marginalized in mainstream texts? And, how do we teach students to ask questions about power and language?

An outgrowth of the broader field of critical pedagogy, which uses critical questioning to examine and interrupt oppressive social and educational practices (Freire, 1970), critical literacy encourages readers to actively analyze texts and grapple with the ways those texts both reflect and inform their broader context. By developing students' critical literacy skills, we are able to prepare them to think like historians as they "read the word and the world" in which they live (Freire, 1970). Justice-oriented teachers use critical literacy to meet broader pedagogical goals of dismantling injustice and inequalities, and investigating ideologies that perpetuate an unjust society (Coffey, 2015). They center the "analysis of the relationship among sociopolitical power, social processes, and the construction of knowledge" (Dover, 2013b, p. 5). Embedded in critical pedagogy is the belief that students should be encouraged to question and challenge the status quo and dominant ways of thinking.

In developing students' critical literacy, we challenge students to question issues of power, so that students can read and analyze texts for hidden agendas. Coffey (2015) explains critical literacy as, "the ability to read texts in an active, reflective manner in order to better understand power, inequality, and injustice in human relationships." Teachers can facilitate the development of students' critical literacy by teaching students to analyze texts for bias and underlying messages, and then challenge students to see the power relations within those messages. A text may be a book, journal, song, television show, magazine article, commercial, or any medium through which individuals are communicating with each other (Freire, 1970). In this way, attaining literacy is not just about preparing students for a technical understanding of how to read, write, and speak, but rather empowering children with "multiple perspectives and questioning habits of mind" (Wolk, 2003, p. 102). When developing students' critical literacy, teachers help students "read between the lines" (Lee, Menkart, & Okazawa-Rey, 2006, p. iv), instead of merely reading the lines. It is in this way that students learn to examine texts from a critical perspective so that they can determine whose voice is included, whose is left out, and why.

Exploring multiple perspectives is a key component of critical literacy. Teachers incorporate multiple perspectives so that students can see texts are biased. When reading a text critically, a teacher might ask her students questions such as: Whose voice is heard? Whose is missing? Why are certain voices silenced in the text? Questions such as these teach students to examine texts for bias, including the Eurocentric viewpoint that is often promoted in textbooks. By incorporating multiple perspectives through multiple texts, students get the chance to see the many viewpoints of a given event. For example, many groups were involved in the building of the transcontinental railroad. Chinese and Indian immigrants worked under brutal conditions, including low pay, to help build the railroad. Mexican Americans contributed to the railroad as well. Although each of these groups contributed to the building of the railroad, their voices are often unheard of in textbooks (Loewen, 2007; Takaki, 2008).

Teaching from the textbook directly, without encouraging students to question and critically think about the messages and assumptions embedded within these texts, may work to perpetuate a harmful storyline which negates the experiences, voices, and presence of people whose acts of resistance and contributions have helped build the country we currently live in (Agarwal-Rangnath, 2013). As Johnson (2007) explains, traditional curriculum often "denies students the opportunity to benefit from the knowledge, perspectives, and understanding to be gained from studying other cultural groups' experiences and attaining the intercultural competency to work with everyone" (p. 146). By intentionally integrating the history and perspectives of all people, and juxtaposing historical text and content against various points of reference and multiple perspectives, students will develop a more critical and comprehensive understanding of the past and present (Zinn, 2003). In social studies, it is particularly important to incorporate multiple perspectives through supplementary material and counter-texts (texts that portray the point of view of a person or group that may be silenced in dominant texts) so that students learn the stories and contributions of people and groups who often remained silenced in our textbook. By incorporating multiple perspectives, we can help students to see that there is more than one story that can be told about any event that happens (Wade, 2007, p. 38). Delving deep into history, through the perspective of those outside of the White norm, we may begin to construct a vision of history that elucidates the achievement, struggles, and acts of resistance as important and integral to the collective creation of society, our country, and our world.

As students critique society and learn to name injustice and inequality through critical literacy, teachers also become facilitators of social change in the classroom. Teachers encourage students to see what is unjust and to take action on their decisions through inquiry, dialogue, and activism. They allow students to see how their daily decisions about how to live can help make a better world. Teachers may also facilitate social change projects in which students find ways to change what they see as unfair or unjust in their school, communities, or society at large. By teaching literacy in this way, teachers help their students to interrogate the world as a text, counter historical myths, think for themselves, and take action on their decisions through inquiry, dialogue, and activism (Wolk, 2003). In this conception, students are conceived as agents of transformation in classrooms, schools, and communities, raising questions of whose knowledge is in the curriculum, and examining the foundations of history (Au, 2009). This creates opportunities for students to learn the technical skills they need to pass pencil-and-paper tests and succeed academically (as measured by standardized tests), and also learn to be critical and active members of society.

As the CCSS focus heavily on literacy skills and not content, history/social studies teachers have the added challenge to step out of their expertise to incorporate the Common Core literacy standards into their existing curriculum and instruction. For some teachers, the emphasis on literacy with the flexibility of teaching content provides them with the opportunity to promote critical literacy and social justice in the classroom. Many of the teachers in this book took advantage of the CCSS's focus on students' literacy skills as an opportunity to prioritize critical literacy in the classroom.

In this section, we spotlight two teachers who incorporate critical literacy into their social studies teaching, Melissa Gibson and Dawn Fontaine. Each teacher facilitates the development of critical literacy in their classrooms, while also finding ways to meet the CCSS.

Melissa's 15 years as an educator include teaching social studies and English to grades 6–12 in both private and public schools in Chicago, Los Angeles, Wisconsin, and Mexico. In addition, Melissa works with Northwestern University's Civic Education Project, leading high school students and faculty in justice-oriented programming around the United States. She holds a PhD in Curriculum and Instruction from the University of Wisconsin, Madison, conducts research on educational and social justice that has appeared in publications such as *Equity & Excellence in Education* and *Multicultural Perspectives*, and has taught both preservice teachers and graduate students at the university level.

Dawn lives and teaches in a midsized, postindustrial city in the Northeast. She has taught for 18 years in the same district, but in many capacities, including charter, alternative, turn around, and traditional public schools. She earned her master's degree in literacy theory, understanding that being able to build these skills in students would serve them more fully than knowing more history. Currently, she is working on a doctoral degree in teacher education and school improvement at the University of Massachusetts in Amherst. Her research focuses on identifying the resiliency skills inherent in her urban students in order to foster them in the teachers she mentors and coaches. She sees her purpose as an educator as creating opportunities by believing in students' capacity to excel.

MOVING FORWARD THROUGH QUESTIONING

In a new classroom with rows of desks and left-behind materials; a year that was supposed to cover feudal Europe, the birth of Islam, and imperial Japan, Melissa struggled to find her bearing in this new context. She sat down with her textbook—*The Medieval World and Beyond*—attempting to figure out what she was supposed to teach.

Melissa encountered numerous challenges in her effort to teach social studies curriculum, including finding ways to meet the day-to-day demands of a classroom teacher and create and enact curriculum that matched her vision of justice-oriented teaching. Melissa shares in her letter:

> I couldn't ignore how students' eyes glazed over as we took notes on feudalism or how they alternated between boredom and mania as we learned about the medieval church. I knew what my supervisor self would say about cultural relevance, social justice, democratic education, active learning. . . . But all of this was pushed aside by what seemed more pressing: How can I get them to stop talking? How can I get them to do their homework? Where are my assessments? And what am I going to teach *tomorrow*?

From this selection, we can see the challenges Melissa encountered as she re-entered the classroom. She leaned on her textbook as a primary source of curriculum, having students take notes from the dominant narrative produced in this mainstream text. She felt conflicted, struggling to find ways to both teach for social justice and meet the day-to-day requirements of teaching. Having taught at the university level, she had prepared and supported teachers to enact justice-oriented curriculum in the classroom. Now, she herself struggled with the daily challenges of teaching, which included curriculum development and classroom management. As she explained in her letter, "It's embarrassing to admit [using the textbook directly], but I share it because I want you to know that I understand: I understand how hard it is to become the teacher you want to be in light of standards and assessments and time demands. I understand—but I also know there is a way forward." Having experienced the trials of being a "new" teacher, Melissa now better understood the challenges of teaching in today's context. In the next section, we hear how Melissa was able to push through her struggles to enact critical literacy in the classroom.

Defining Critical Literacy

As Melissa struggled in her next context, she found a way forward through questioning. To her, literacy in a traditional social studies classroom appeared too often about the passive intake of text: being able to repeat a historical storyline and its accompanying details. In traditional social studies literacy, the critical questioning of text is not often emphasized. Students are not often encouraged to ask, "Can I trust this source/textbook? Whose story is this, anyways? Whose voice is missing?" Instead, they are encouraged to commit to memory the official stories of history and the social sciences.

Melissa argues that stories—especially those in history, which carry the weight of official facts for students—are not neutral. She explains:

> Stories are the filters through which we make sense of our world. But as Paolo Freire argued, the heart of a critical education is "reading the world," which students are usually hungering to do so. By emphasizing critical literacy over rote comprehension, we help students develop the tools to do so. Rather than encourage the blind absorption of information, critical literacy demands that students constantly assess trustworthiness, bias, perspective. It asks students to compare sources, to challenge narratives, to compile evidence, and to construct arguments. It helps students to begin to see the "master narratives" linking texts—narratives implicated in the reproduction of privilege and inequity. It teaches students to triangulate data, to seek multiple sources and perspective, and to practice communicating to diverse audiences. Especially in today's media-saturated world, where inaccuracies and propaganda go viral as "facts" and where Facebook has become a primary news source, students need to be able to pause and say, "Wait a minute. That story doesn't make sense. What about . . . ?" If students are going to read the world—if they are going to reconcile their lived experience with the words on the page—they've got to be able to think critically about those words and not just spout them back as lists of historical information.

Melissa further explains that the storylines portrayed in textbooks such as Columbus as a hero, Africa as a backwards and inferior continent, more as always better, racism and slavery as historical anomalies, and Europeans as providers of light and progress to the world, become the official storylines students come to learn. For Melissa, the "storylines in textbooks are not just inaccuracies; they are narrative acts of aggression." She explains that critical literacy is one essential tool for interrupting this aggression. When a teacher works to develop critical literacy in her students, she is not just providing an alternative storyline that students are expected to remember, but rather she is equipping her students with the skills they need to critically question the world.

Critical Literacy in Practice

To facilitate questioning in the classroom and develop students' critical literacy skills, Melissa challenged students to question what they read. Prior, she had students read and take notes directly from the textbook, and now students were expected to analyze their textbook for bias. As she explains in her letter:

> At the front of my room was a poster, a reminder of how I wanted to teach: *A Critical Historian's Essential Questions.* Whose voice is missing? Can I trust this source? Where is the bias? How would this (hi)story be different if told from another perspective? What is the evidence? Is this a logical conclusion based on that evidence? How does this connect to the world today?

When I found us yet again taking notes, I started asking questions: Whose voice is missing in our textbook's version of feudalism? My students struggled with the idea that a textbook had a voice, so we probed differently: What is the bias in this version? Here, they had some hunches, such as Daniela saying that serfs would not have found this system of servitude as beneficial as the textbook claimed. We pushed deeper: How would this history be different if told from another perspective? Our exploration became a writing assignment where students assumed the identity of a member of a feudal society and responded to the textbook's claims. As we shared our writing, we returned to that first question, "Whose voice is missing?" and its corollary, "Whose perspective does this represent?" My students began to see how even "authorities" like textbooks can represent a limited perspective.

Melissa believed that by interrogating the assigned curriculum, she was opening up space for her students to think more critically about history. She may not be teaching about social justice issues yet, but she was getting her students to see that texts could be written from multiple perspectives. To her, this was critical literacy and "a core piece of teaching for social justice."

Melissa continued to facilitate the development of critical literacy in her students by using lessons from *Rethinking Columbus* to teach about perspective. She introduced students to conflicting versions of Columbus's expedition. Students read primary sources (e.g., Columbus's journals), secondary sources (e.g., excerpts from *A People's History of the US*), and fictionalized accounts (Jane Yolen's *Encounter*). She then had students retell "this well-worn piece of history" from different perspectives in a dialectic journal. In a dialectic journal, two voices respond to one another's reflections. Usually, a prompt or question is assigned; one voice answers and then shares his or her writing with a partner, who responds. The two voices can go back and forth indefinitely, having a thoughtful written dialogue on a probing question. For Melissa, the case of Columbus helped her students see how a text can have a voice that inevitably represents a limited perspective. Coinciding with Columbus Day, she also had students practice building an argument with evidence by writing an editorial addressing the question, *Should we celebrate Columbus as a hero*?

Melissa's first attempts at teaching social studies were limited to the textbook, but she was able to move forward by integrating critical literacy into her teaching. She began by having students question bias in their textbooks and ask important questions such as whose voice and perspective is missing from the excerpts. She then had students examine and explore conflicting readings around Columbus's expedition. Last, Melissa had students turn to Chimamanda Adichie's TED talk, "The Danger of a Single Story" to consider the bias in news coverage. Each of these activities asked students to think critically about the texts they encountered. Students learned to question what they read, understand and see bias, and see and name what perspectives and voices are missing and why.

Learning to enact justice-oriented social studies curriculum in the classroom is not easy. Melissa shared with us the challenges she faced in re-entering the classroom; many of these challenges might be synonymous with what you might be experiencing when learning to teach in an era of the Common Core. For Melissa, "knowing and understanding the challenges of implementing critical, social justice-oriented curriculum in her classroom" was essential to her being able to move forward. As she better understood the constraints of the classroom, she found ways to navigate the challenges by enacting lessons that developed students' critical literacy. She believed critical literacy to be a key component of social justice teaching.

As Melissa came to understand the "quicksand of demands" that can so easily bog down one's practice, in her letter she shared a list of suggestions to help teachers navigate the challenges of the classroom. Below are her suggestions:

- *Show your students that you are a critical historian and social scientist.* Those critical questions on the poster in my room? Those are the questions *I* ask whenever I read history. Apprentice your students into your thinking process: Use metacognitive strategies to show your students how you critique textbook history, and then give them a chance to practice. This is an essential starting point when working with an assigned curriculum.
- *Critical questioning is the heart of teaching for social justice.* Social studies "best practices" are built on questioning—essential questions in unit planning, big questions in research. So, too, is justice-oriented teaching. If you center your work on critical questions—whether a set list of analysis questions, unit-specific essential questions, or student-developed questions—you will be cultivating a critical lens on the social sciences.
- *Questions lead to questions; be willing to get "off track."* Critical work requires that you deviate from "the plan." Maybe it's something "extra" you identify, such as my unit on perspective, or maybe it's a tangent to which your students lead you. Regardless, allowing for spontaneous, layered discoveries allows us to develop the thinking skills and knowledge base required of critically conscious citizens.
- *Using your resources to ease the burden of this work.* Because of *Rethinking Schools* and the Zinn Education Project, I was aware of *Rethinking Columbus*. Because of my work with the Global Nomads Group, I had access to an alternative curriculum on critical literacy, already aligned with the Common Core. I also use the National Council of the Social Studies to support my work philosophically and concretely. Joining communities of and talking to like-minded educators will make it easier to move beyond Chapter 1.
- *Let students lead.* As critical questioning becomes part of your practice, students may be eager to direct the course of study. We want students to become competent thinkers, so let them ask and answer their own questions—about your curriculum, about global issues, about perspective and bias. Today, my

> course (8th-grade U.S. Civics) revolves around the Social Issues Research and Action Project, a student-directed project where students pose and answer questions about pressing social issues.

Melissa advises teachers, "to grasp the courage it takes to step away from the textbook." Her insightful suggestions, as well as thought-provoking activities around bias, help us to consider how one can promote critical literacy in the classroom. For Melissa, CCSS is an opportunity for her to reclaim her teaching, as she sees the CCSS as supportive of her work. With the focus on literacy skills and not content, Melissa is able to infuse features of critical literacy into her teaching, while still addressing the social studies content she is expected to teach.

EXAMINING BIAS AND PERSPECTIVE

Dawn describes teaching as a "rewarding profession where in one school day you can experience the purest joy and deepest frustrations." For Dawn, teaching for social justice comes with its ups and downs. When working to challenge a system that is unjust, she explains that you might be left feeling like you "are operating in conflicting worlds." Sometimes the work of educating young people through social justice pedagogy will feel encouraging and inspiring, while other days you may lose hope when change seems impossible. As a social justice educator, she sees her job as a seed planter. As she describes, "we should not be looking to harvest the fruit; when we do, we become frustrated that there is no fruit to harvest. Take your responsibility of a seed planter seriously and with great honor and be content." Dawn advises teachers to find a balance between challenging and questioning, and take away what works for you.

Defining Critical Literacy

In Dawn's mind, there are many ways to think about a pedagogy informed by social justice. She explains teaching for social justice as the following:

> One acknowledges and incorporates multiple voices and perspectives, especially those that are underrepresented in standard curriculum; shares power inherent in the dynamics of teaching and learning; acts as an ally; questions; and understands

> the larger social, political, economic and historical contexts that frame the lives of their students.

Dawn sees each of the above aspects of social justice teaching as important and integral to her work as a justice-oriented educator. When thinking about creating and enacting curriculum in the classroom, Dawn draws on Freirean critical literacy as a key aspect of her justice-oriented teaching. She describes her vision for justice-oriented social studies teaching below:

> Showing students how to identify perspective, then determine what they think about it. Every historical event, speech and act is interpreted in multiple ways through multiple perspectives.

A key aspect of critical literacy for Dawn is incorporating multiple texts into her teaching so that students have the opportunity to critique the perspectives and values that are being promoted. As Dawn develops students' critical literacy through the analysis of perspective in texts, she also teaches students to see the bias in their own perspectives, as our own perspective is influenced by our life experiences. She uses the following African proverb, "Until the lions have their historians, tales of hunting will always glorify the hunter" as a touchstone text, which she repeatedly comes back to when discussing the notion of perspective. Dawn believes this African proverb clearly elucidates what she wants her students to understand about perspective. This being, "what rises to the surface are the perspectives that are valued by the dominant culture." In other words, mainstream texts tend to privilege the voices of dominant culture, while silencing the voices of those traditionally marginalized. Dawn facilitates the development of critical literacy in her students by asking them to question whose voices or experiences are missing from the perspective represented in a textbook, video, or other curricular resource and why. Further, she has students critically examine historical interpretations. As students analyze the interpretation, she asks students to consider whose voice might be missing from the interpretation and how the interpretation of the historical event might look different if it was written from another perspective. By challenging students to question texts, she believes that her students learn that each of them have the right and responsibility to ask questions. Students also learn the valuable life skill of empathy through the study of multiple perspectives. In this way, students are able to understand how others influence our lives.

Additionally, students may begin to see that the voices valued in textbooks and other dominant texts are those that portray a Eurocentric perspective. Voices that are silenced or minimally presented are most often the voices of traditionally marginalized groups.

As Dawn challenges students to examine perspective, she also sees the study of language and power to be a key element of critical literacy. She wants her students to understand the unfair privileging of dominant discourses and engage students in conversations about this issue, while also empowering students to see how and where they can use their voice. She hopes to provide students with the tools they need to access and navigate dominant culture. In this way, Dawn aims to provide students with the tools that they need to name and critique the injustices and inequalities of our world, and also find ways to use their literacies to participate in their communities to make change. By developing students' critical literacy, Dawn feels she is empowering her students to impact the world that influences them daily.

Critical Literacy in the Classroom

In this next section, we share a 2-day lesson plan written and implemented by Dawn in her classroom. The lessons attend to the values and practices Dawn regards as critical literacy.

In Dawn's first lesson, she aims for students to discuss the varying impacts of the caste system in India by annotating two videos. She begins the lesson introducing the notion of social hierarchy through a series of discussion questions: Why do all social groups have a hierarchy? Why do some people have more power than others? Why does power influence some people to abuse it? After students have had a chance to discuss these questions in detail, she then furthers her students thinking around social hierarchy by asking the following: What might be the pros and cons of a social structure where there was total equality? After students share their answers, she has students watch two YouTube videos about ancient India and its caste system.

After students have seen the two videos, Dawn asks them to share what they learned about the caste system. She then asks them to consider how the caste system is similar or different to European feudalism and Japanese feudalism, the other two social structures they have learned about. Dawn concludes the lesson with the following discussion question: Do you think a caste-based social structure might help or hurt Indian society?

In the second part of the lesson, Dawn intends for students to reflect on the experiences of the lower classes in the caste system. She begins the discussion by asking students questions such as: Why do all social groups have a hierarchy? Why do some people have more power than others? And why does power influence some people to abuse it?

Next, Dawn does a read aloud of the book, *A Taste of Freedom: Gandhi and the Great Salt March* (Kimmel, 2014), while students take notes about the experience of the main character. After reading the book, students write/pair/share to the question: How do the character's experiences and beliefs intersect with what you know about social hierarchy, specifically the caste system?

After the read aloud, Dawn asks students to do a document-based question (DBQ) and hands out four different documents for students to analyze. DBQs were first used in 1973 as part of the Advanced Placement test in U.S. history, and were designed to assess students' ability to analyze and evaluate diverse primary source texts. DBQs are authentic assessments in which students are asked to read and analyze historical records, synthesize information from different documents, and then respond to an assigned task. In this case, Dawn has students analyze the following documents, which consist of quotes and/or excerpts from books:

Document A: *Taste of Freedom: Gandhi and the Great Salt March* (Kimmel, 2014)

Gandhi's famous Salt March shook the foundations of the British Empire and the world, showing the strength of a people united in peace to fight for freedom. Gandhi's march had a significant effect on changing world and British attitudes towards Indian independence, and inspired the use of nonviolence in other protest movements, like the U.S. Civil Rights Movement. You'll never forget Elizabeth Cody Kimmel's heartwarming, insightful account or Guiliano Ferri's stunning illustrations of the event seen through the eyes of a child inspired by Gandhi's vision for a better world.

Document B: "The best way to find yourself is to lose yourself in the service of others."

"Power is of two kinds. One is obtained by the fear of punishment and the other by acts of love. Power based on love is a thousand times more effective and permanent then the one derived from fear of punishment." —Mahatma Gandhi

Document C: Examining the social structure of India

According to Hindu religion, the first man, Manu Svayambhuva, laid down the laws by which people were to live. These laws, the Code of Manu, divided Hindu society into four social classes: the Brahmins were the priests and wise men; the kshatriyas were the warriors; the Vaisyas were the merchants (traders) and farmers; and the Shudras were the menial (unskilled) laborers. The following excerpt from the Code of Manu states that each social class was to have its own set of duties and rules, or dharma.

> If a man of one birth assaults one of the twice-born castes with virulent (poisonous) words, he ought to have his tongue cut, for he is of the lowest origin (class). If a low-born (low class) man endeavors (undertakes) to sit down by the side of a high-born (high class) man, he should be banished after being branded on the hip, or the king may cause his backside to be cut off. "Gandhi and the satyagrhis are ready to leave by dawn. I join a long line of people as the Mahatma begins walking. His pace is very fast. Even Rajiv has to breathe heavily to keep up."

Document D: "All tyranny needs to gain a foothold is for people of good conscience to remain silent." —Thomas Jefferson.

After students have had time to read through each document, she asks students to work through the following questions:

- Document A: Why might people with less power not fight back?
- Document B & C: What is the central idea of this text?
- Document C: How does Gandhi's quote apply to what you think about the purpose of social structure?
- Document D: Jefferson is giving a warning—how does it connect to our thinking about social structure?

Dawn leads students in a discussion around the questions. She then ends the lesson having students do a reflection exercise, in which students compare and contrast the three social systems they have studied thus far: European feudalism, Japanese feudalism, and the caste system of India.

Through the 2-day lesson plan, Dawn feels she is able to attend to the values and practices of critical literacy in a few ways. First, she believes she was able to develop students' critical literacy by explicitly teaching students the language of power. In Dawn's mind, she believes that to be heard in academic and professional spaces in the United States, one needs to know the language terms and structure of that discourse. Building the space for discussion in students' own language, and then reshaping those ideas into academic language values, gives students a chance to see the role of time, place, and audience when it comes to selecting which language to use. Second, she explains that all of the texts selected for the two lessons were designed to provoke questioning, which is at the core of critical literacy. Dawn feels that when a classroom culture is shaped by critical literacy, teachers and students alike are empowered to question. These questions drive a quest for knowledge and action. Specifically, in these lessons, students question the relationships among groups in a social hierarchy influenced by power. Third, Dawn feels she draws on features of critical literacy as the activities were designed to tap into students' empathy. Asking students to do a comparison, to think about a causal relationship, and/or to interpret pros and cons creates space for interrogating the text and contributing their own emerging knowledge.

Dawn's lesson on the caste system of India was centered on questioning. She asked students to examine and critique the structure of social hierarchies, while also challenging students to consider which groups may benefit or be hurt by such social structures. She then connects students' understanding around the caste system to previous studies of social structures so that students could draw connections between the three social systems they have studies thus far. Dawn also integrated multiple texts, outside of the textbook, for students to deconstruct. The supplemental texts provided students with the opportunity to hear the voices of those who may be silenced or marginalized in mainstream texts.

Dawn sees the CCSS as an opportunity to embrace her justice-oriented teaching. She was able to meet Common Core standards and develop students' critical literacy through her lessons on the caste system. For example, this specific lesson met CCSS.ELA-Literacy. RH.9-10.2: Determine the central ideas or information of a primary or secondary source. Dawn sees the CCSS as an opportunity for her to teach students about language and power, engage students in a study of history from multiple perspectives, and develop students' ability to deconstruct texts so that they can see whose knowledge is being privileged.

CONCLUSION

As we discussed in this chapter, justice-oriented teachers can develop students' critical literacy by asking students to examine bias in texts and take note of whose voice is portrayed in the account and whose is not. To integrate the voices of those that may be silenced or missing from the description, we can present different pieces of literature that portray the points of view of groups that are traditionally marginalized in mainstream texts. We can also lean on supplementary texts, such as primary and secondary sources, outside literature, films, guest speakers, and so forth, to provide students with a more ample account of the event than what might be portrayed in a textbook. By presenting these multiple perspectives, students' misconceptions around history may be challenged. Students are given the opportunity to act like historians as they grapple with multiple texts that portray multiple perspectives. As students examine texts for bias, they may find intersections and contradictions between texts to formulate their own historical interpretations.

By allowing the voices of those silenced to enter the mainstream narrative, students may see history in a different light. They will learn the stories of those who struggled to overcome discrimination and racism, who fought to make change so future generations could find peace in a better world. Students may feel inspired and empowered to hear how their ancestors fought against discrimination, racism, and oppression to make change in our world. Through the exploration of multiple perspectives, students may see that our country was built by the complex contributions of many groups, not just the ones listed in our textbooks.

In this chapter, we witnessed Melissa and Dawn's efforts toward developing students' critical literacy in the classroom. Melissa's first attempts at teaching social studies were limited to the textbook, but she was able to move forward by integrating critical literacy into her teaching. She developed students' critical literacy by having students question bias in their textbooks, examine and explore conflicting readings around Columbus's expedition, and watch Chimamanda

Adichie's TED talk, "The Danger of a Single Story," to explore the bias in news coverage. In each of these activities, Melissa was challenging her students to think critically about the texts, question what they read, and consider whose perspective might be missing and why.

In Dawn's classroom, students explored the caste system of India. Dawn had students question the structures of power and hierarchy within the caste system by asking students to explore how relationships exist within this type of social structure and how they might compare to other social structures they have studied. Dawn provided students with multiple contexts, including YouTube videos, quotes, and stories, outside of the traditional textbook curriculum to explore and learn about the caste system of India. For Dawn, teaching students to question is a key feature of critical literacy. Dawn believes that critical literacy is empowering students to see multiple perspectives and analyze text for bias.

Both Melissa and Dawn found ways to enact justice-oriented teaching in the classroom and still meet the CCSS. They each used questioning as a key component of their lessons. Questioning is a skill that is directly built into the CCSS and also a key feature of critical literacy. For example, if we look at the English Language Arts and History/Social Studies standards for grades 6–8, each of these standards could be met through critical literacy questions.

Key Ideas and Details:

CCSS.ELA-LITERACY.RH.6-8.1

Cite specific textual evidence to support analysis of primary and secondary sources.

CCSS.ELA-LITERACY.RH.6-8.2

Determine the central ideas or information of a primary or secondary source; provide an accurate summary of the source distinct from prior knowledge or opinions.

CCSS.ELA-LITERACY.RH.6-8.3

Identify key steps in a text's description of a process related to history/social studies (e.g., how a bill becomes law, how interest rates are raised or lowered).

Craft and Structure:

CCSS.ELA-LITERACY.RH.6-8.4

Determine the meaning of words and phrases as they are used in a text, including vocabulary specific to domains related to history/social studies.

CCSS.ELA-LITERACY.RH.6-8.5

Describe how a text presents information (e.g., sequentially, comparatively, causally).

CCSS.ELA-LITERACY.RH.6-8.6

Identify aspects of a text that reveal an author's point of view or purpose (e.g., loaded language, inclusion or avoidance of particular facts).

With the shift to the CCSS, teachers may be struggling to find ways to align their instruction with the new standards and uphold their commitment to justice-oriented teaching. Melissa and Dawn remind us that this is possible, as they exemplify how one can meet standards and develop students' critical literacy, a core piece of teaching for social justice.

The CCSS expects students will be able to attain literacy skills such as determining the central idea of a text. One can meet this standard by asking students a teacher-directed comprehension question such as, "what is the main idea?" or take a critical literacy approach and instead ask questions which challenge students to delve deeper. Students would still be engaging in a close reading of the text, which is what the CCSS calls for, but would alternatively be challenged to analyze the text for the hidden messages and bias.

Papola (2013) offers examples of critical literacy questions one could use to analyze texts:

- Whose voices are heard and whose are silenced?
- Who is privileged and who is marginalized in the text?
- What does the author want us to think?
- How does the author use specific language to promote his or her beliefs?
- What action might you take based on what you have learned from the text?

Papola (2013) argues that critical literacy questions (such as the ones listed above), "go way beyond the simple who, what, where, when, why format of questioning as suggested in the CCSS, but allow students to answer those same types of questions in the process." In other words, when we are working to develop students' critical literacy, we are preparing them to be able to answer any text-based comprehension question, including complex critical literacy questions that relate to who is promoted and who is silenced in texts. As history/social studies teachers face the increased pressure to step out of their area of expertise to incorporate the Common Core literacy standards into their existing curriculum and instruction, critical literacy is a potential pathway for teachers to integrate literacy standards into their teaching. Students learn to deconstruct texts from a critical lens, interrogate multiple viewpoints, and analyze texts for language and power. These critical literacy strategies serve to make our students think like historians and be strong, analytical, and empowered readers.

CHAPTER 4

"What Will I Teach?"

Justice-Oriented Content for Critical Hope

> Good social justice social studies teachers are committed to developing content that explicitly addresses issues of injustice (e.g., sexism, racism, ableism, homophobia, classism, and economic inequality, etc.) while simultaneously keeping track of how practices and policies within the school may be creating or exacerbating inequalities.
>
> —Katy Swalwell

Before the beginning of each school year, every teacher is faced with the important content-focused curricular question, "What will I teach?" Embedded within this question are the corollary questions, "What do I *want* to teach?" and "What am I *supposed* to teach?" For most justice-oriented teachers in accountability-driven classrooms, the numerous answers to these two questions often do not match, especially those related to social studies content (Agarwal, 2011; Au, 2009).

As we read in Chapters 1 and 2, the tension between what these teachers believe their students should learn, know, and be able to do, and what local, state, and federal governments believe they should, is an important one to address and seek resolution to. Thankfully, despite the continued dominance of secondary social studies textbooks and ready-made resources that perpetuate dominant (and limited) historical narratives, and corresponding content standards that marginalize the lived experiences of the vast majority of human beings (Grant & Sleeter, 2011), justice-oriented teachers continue to build, curate, and prioritize justice-oriented history and social studies *content* for their students.

In this chapter, we provide guidance from our veteran teachers and related educational research on how one might be successful in this regard. We will also use examples from three veteran teachers' curriculum to illustrate content-driven strategies for teaching to social justice topics and themes in history and contemporary society. Now, in so doing, and following this with a chapter that focuses on justice-oriented pedagogical approaches, we do not intend to set up a dichotomy between content and pedagogy. What a teacher teaches and how/why they teach should be interrelated propositions. It is with this tension that Chapters 4 and 5 are written. Our veteran teachers spoke of the importance of both content and pedagogy being interwoven and interdependent, but we have separated them here to focus our attention on these components as at least somewhat different from one another and worthy of separate discussion.

JUSTICE-ORIENTED CONTENT

In examining our teachers' advice on the topic of content, most highlighted the need to develop content that "explicitly addresses issues of injustice," as Katy states above. In defining content, it is important to think about the nature and/or amount of information we want students to examine or learn. In Chapter 3 on critical literacy, we described the importance of having students examine more than just the story (or stories) presented in a class textbook, but also/instead provide texts that present multiple perspectives, of historically silenced voices, of contrasting viewpoints of the same events. In Wade's eight-element framework for a social justice education (2001), two come to mind as helping us to assess what might be considered justice-oriented content: *analytical* and *intellectual*. According to Wade, social justice teachers ask students to critique the status quo, examine underlying assumptions and values, and explore their own roles in relation to social issues. They also consider whose voices are left out, who makes the decisions, whose stories are buried, and how to create change as they uncover various sources of information. In the end, *analyzing* the causes of injustice in the school, community, society, and world is at the heart of social justice education.

The selection of these focal texts requires that teachers think deeply about the rigor and richness of the material, and that teachers have well-developed content knowledge themselves. As another of Wade's elements, *intellectual*, reminds us, social justice education involves real intellectual work on the part of students and teachers. For many new social studies teachers, prioritizing content is a significant challenge, as the breadth of social studies courses, and the hundreds of standards listed that they are told to "cover" is overwhelming. In addition, it is of equal importance that they continually interrogate the racist, classist, and sexist assumptions likely present in their courses (Cochran-Smith, 2000). There is good news though: We get to keep learning.

DEVELOP YOUR CONTENT KNOWLEDGE ALWAYS

Justice-oriented teachers realize that they are continually deepening their fluency in the content they already teach, and are constantly seeking to expand the breadth of their knowledge base. So, teachers don't need to know everything, or pretend they do. For example, as his classes begin a unit, Brian stacks all of the many readings, books, photographs, and DVDs on the front and sides of his desk to show how much study went into the unit, and how much he continues to do to make it even richer. These piles often reach unsafe heights! Sarah Lundy, in sharing with students her passion about history, models what she hopes her students will do or become:

> I became a social studies teacher because I am genuinely curious about the enduring questions that historians, political scientists, and economists pursue. Every significant social justice issue has gnarled historical roots, tangled economic motivations, and heartbreaking social implications. Whether I am adhering tightly to prescribed content or choosing content with enormous latitude, my approach is the same. I establish my own relationship with the content. I research. I read. I listen to experts speak about their work. I develop my own intellectual intimacy with historical figures and pivotal turning points, with political trends, with driving economic forces. While I'm immersed in the content, I pay attention to what surprises me, to what confuses me, and to when my heartstrings are tugged fiercely enough to snap.

In addition to earning advanced degrees in education and in the social sciences (which many did, despite their already resource-intense professional lives), the veteran teachers also capitalized on the fantastic low-cost resources, support, and professional development provided regularly by national organizations like Facing History and Ourselves (see www.facinghistory.org), Zinn Education Project (see zinnedproject.org), Teaching Tolerance (see www.tolerance.org), and Rethinking Schools (see www.rethinkingschools.org).

STAY LOCAL AND CURRENT

Additionally, in this intellectual search for justice-oriented content, teachers may not have to look very far. A clear piece of advice was to tap into local histories, community knowledge, current events, and student culture to choose content that would best engage them. Isabel and her students together explored data showing that a new school building had not been built in their population-dense urban community for generations. They then wrote heartfelt written appeals to the public to show that they deserved such a new school, counter to negative media portrayals of them as hoodlums and gangbangers. At her school, Laura thought to recruit her students and their family members as teachers of history:

> The father of one of my Afghan students can do a far better job than I can in teaching about recent history of his country, the Cambodian priest of another one of my students deeply touched my class in telling his experience during the genocide, and my student's interview of his grandfather is a far more vibrant picture of Mexican history than I could provide.

Also, our veteran teachers used the Internet to great advantage, as have many other justice-oriented educators, where in reaction to current events such as those in Ferguson in 2014 until the present, online resource repositories and syllabi have been created for public use and education (see #FergusonSyllabus at bit.ly/FergusonSyllabus and Teaching Ferguson at jupsteachingferguson.wordpress.com/2014/09/05/teaching-resources). These crowdsourced and free resources create a rich, living text of things happening right now to draw from, with a variety of perspectives and untold histories to be shared (Rubin, 2011, 2015).

INTRODUCTION TO FOCUS TEACHERS

In this chapter, we spotlight three teachers who effectively incorporate justice-oriented social studies content into their teaching: Brian Gibbs, Laura Einhorn, and Jared Kushida. Each of them take unique approaches to teaching and learning with their students in standards-aligned social studies classrooms, and have refined processes for both making choices about what content to teach, and how to deal with mandated content. Their teaching includes justice-oriented content, they work continually to develop their content knowledge, and bring the study of history to a local and current focus. At their respective schools, they are considered to be accomplished practitioners by school leadership, their colleagues, and the communities they serve in East Los Angeles and Oakland/East Bay. In what remains of this chapter, we will ask two questions of their teaching practice: "How do you decide what to teach?" and "How do you deal with mandated content?"

Brian Gibbs taught world history, U.S. history, and American government at Theodore Roosevelt High School in East Los Angeles for 16 years and has been a teacher educator at various universities for 15 years. Currently a nonpracticing history teacher, he is pursuing a doctorate in the Department of Curriculum and Instruction at the University of Wisconsin–Madison. He will be moving to North Carolina in the coming academic year to take a tenure track faculty position at the University of North Carolina at Chapel Hill.

Laura is entering her 7th year of teaching history at KIPP King Collegiate High School in San Lorenzo, CA, a community located between Oakland and Hayward. She teaches or has taught a number of courses, including world history, humanities, and a 12th-grade seminar course she developed herself. She also serves as the faculty advisor to the King DREAM club to support undocumented students. Moreover, she is the advisor of the Social Justice Club, a student-driven group advocating for food and environmental justice, leading conversations about feminism, and championing antibullying work. In addition to teaching at the same high school for the last 7 years, Laura and Jared recently married one another.

Jared is a dedicated and passionate social studies teacher of 11 years, teaching courses such as U.S. History, War & Peace, Ancient and Modern World History, and Geography. He started his career at Azusa High School in Azusa, CA, where he spent 4 years, created the student club Social Awareness for Everyone (SAFE) and then moved to the Bay Area to join the 2nd-year staff at KIPP King Collegiate. Jared has designed the curriculum for U.S. History and War & Peace courses, and he continues to overhaul and innovate them. According to Jared, progressive and critical education means everything to him, as do his students, to whom he owes all his respect and love.

HOW DO YOU DECIDE WHAT TO TEACH?

Laura: "I ask questions"

I teach history specifically because I believe that our conventional telling of history strips away the agency and humanity of

> people of color, the poor, women, people of different religious backgrounds, people from other countries (especially "non-western" countries), people who are gender queer, disabled, etc.
> —Laura Einhorn

In Chapter 2, we introduced Laura and described how she took advantage of the social studies content-based "leeway" provided by the CCSS to develop a 12th-grade elective seminar course titled, "Race, Class, Gender, and Sexuality" (RCGS). In this course, she focused on CCSS literacy skills like "evaluating authors' different points of view on the same historical event or issue" among others. But, instead of practicing these skills by comparing the Federalist Papers and Adam Smith's *Wealth of Nations* to each other, she chose more current voices like Ta-Nehisi Coates and his "The Case for Reparations" and Kevin Williamson's response to it in the *National Review*. To enact a justice-oriented pedagogy, how does Laura choose these more current sources of content, which are arguably more relatable to her students' lives and present context? When sitting down to write a unit plan or lesson plan, there are a number of questions and factors that guide Laura's thinking around her choices on content:

- What academic standards are we working toward?
- What is happening in our community, our state, our nation, and the globe that is shaping our experiences or the experiences of others?
- Which anchor texts and materials can I choose to marry what's happening in our community with the academic standards I want to target?
- What's going on in my students' lives?
- How old are my students?

In this next section, we explore how Laura uses these questions, one by one, by sharing the creative process behind her Identity and Relevance unit in the RCGS seminar course.

What academic standards are we working toward?

If Laura feels her students have clearly mastered identifying an author's claim and supporting evidence, but need work inferring why the author chose to include a particular rhetorical device, that is the focus she will create for them. Laura believes her students need to be strong readers, writers, thinkers, and communicators. Although important, the development of a critical consciousness won't get them anywhere if they can't get past the various gatekeepers of academia.

What's happening in our community, our state, our nation, and the globe that's shaping our experiences or the experiences of others?

Over the Thanksgiving break of 2014, Bob McCulloch and a grand jury failed to indict Darren Wilson, a White police officer in Ferguson, MO, for the murder of Michael Brown, an unarmed African American teenager. President Obama also announced his intention to shield five million undocumented immigrants from deportation. Laura felt there was nothing else to do but spend the last weekend of their break furiously reading, learning, and finding resources to share with her class. Also, when she collects articles to read and videos to watch, she is transparent with them about the bias of various media sources and her own lens and philosophy. Laura believes critical media literacy is a vital 21st-century skill and a daunting task in the era when only a closely discerning eye can detect the differences between articles/posts in the *Huffington Post* versus the *National Review*.

Which anchor texts and materials can I choose to marry what's happening in our community with the academic standards I want to target?

In Laura's view, there are so many rich and well-crafted books and articles that make up the new cannon of social justice studies. She has found Michele Alexander's *The New Jim Crow*, Matt Taibbi's *The Divide*, and anything by Ta-Nehisi Coates and Jonathan Katz to be invaluable in crafting a shared understanding of society. Documentary films, including "Hip Hop: Beyond Beats and Rhymes" by Byron Hurt, "The House I Live In" by Eugene Jarecki, and "Precious Knowledge" by Ari Palos also provide a memorable learning experience to anchor or supplement text.

What's going on in my students' lives?

Laura's students in RCGS are graduating seniors. As a result, last year they ended up spending almost a month deconstructing California's laws around sexual consent and rape culture: a very pressing concern for college-bound kids. Laura's scope and sequence doesn't always allow for this type of flexibility, but she always wants to be responsive to what her students want and need to learn about.

How old are my students?

To Laura, another huge consideration is whether or not content is developmentally appropriate for her students. In addition to teaching 12th-grade RCGS, she also teaches a 9th-grade ancient world history course. When the #BlackandBrownlivesmatter club at her school urged all teachers to hold a day-long teach-in on police brutality, she thought hard about what content would be accessible to her 9th-grade students. Of course, her students watch TV, go online, and live in a community with a deep-seated social consciousness. That said, Laura wasn't sure that too much too soon about understanding systems of oppression was the correct approach with 9th graders. She doesn't want to shield her students from the truth and couldn't if she tried. In her words, "they live this injustice and feel it in their DNA." But she feels she must also remember that they are young people at an age where they deserve and need to be emotionally protected.

For her 9th graders, she wrote a lesson on how the media characterized Black victims as dangerous but White killers as troubled or disturbed. She chose this content because it was concrete and rooted in the study of media. Her background is at the high-school level so she posed this question to a number of elementary and middle school teachers she deeply respects, "How do you teach social justice to the little kids?" She received thoughtful answers that included having students share their own experiences, interview community members, and explore concrete narratives and case studies from civil rights leaders. In her view, these entry points are great for any age group.

Jared: "I look to my checklist"

> In *The Matrix,* Morpheus confronts Neo with a choice: To take the Red Pill or the Blue Pill. The Red Pill represents truth, the painful, inconvenient, unforgiving truth. If he takes the Red Pill, Neo would begin on a long and arduous journey to fight against injustice and do whatever it takes to serve his people. On the other hand, the Blue Pill represents blissful, comfortable, easy ignorance. If he takes the Blue Pill, Neo would theoretically return to his cushy world, where he does not educate himself, does not question anything, never fights against injustice, nor stands for his people. It is a classic, fundamental choice: Painful path to truth, versus easy path to ignorance. —Jared Kushida

In Jared's letter of advice, among other things, he felt it was important that he remain true to what he states as his teaching philosophy: a philosophy he sits down at the beginning of each academic year and rewrites. In fact, to keep himself accountable to this philosophy when creating/revising curriculum and choosing content, he created what he calls a Transformative Curriculum Checklist. Of the 11 key characteristics/guiding questions it lists, if he can't answer them positively and convincingly, he goes back and works on making his curriculum more transformative. In this list, there is an array of pedagogical, methodological, and philosophical commitments that Jared is making, and social studies content to be chosen that supports them.

Transformative Curriculum Checklist

I should seek to make my curriculum:

- Truthful—Is this a "Red Pill" lesson?
- Content Heavy—Is the historical information in this lesson plentiful and relevant?
- Critical—Are students going to analyze, evaluate, and question enough?
- Dialectical—Are students going to have the space to dialogue about their ideas?
- Problem-Posing—Are students going to solve a problem that can be related to the real world?
- For community—Does this lesson bring us together? Can what we learn be applied locally?
- Humanizing—Does this historical lesson do justice and restore dignity to the people we are studying?
- Democratizing—Will students have and feel the freedom to make choices?
- Empowering—Can this lead to social justice action in the future?
- Not "Nice"—Does this lesson avoid sugarcoating reality?
- For Hope—Is the idea of possibility present in this lesson?

To Jared, his list stands in stark contrast to usual teaching rubrics and continuums that shortcut teacher preparation programs keep advertising as "best practice." These "teaching recipes" tend to be dropped on new teachers as they practice their craft in full classrooms of students. Then the teachers try to check off elements of "good teaching," such as behavior management strategies, talk time ratio,

SLANTing, and how "joyful" they appear in front of students. While some of these ingredients are necessary to being an effective teacher, ultimately this cookie cutter approach to teaching teachers focuses too much on methods, and pays no attention to the creation and implementation of critical, progressive pedagogy. It prioritizes strategy over purpose, tactics over mission, management over risk, and status quo over transformation. So Jared believes he must do both: commit to his purpose and philosophy, while at the same time being a great methodologist.

Brian: "I teach thematically"

> What does it serve students to learn about the racism, classism, and gendered genocidal past if they don't also learn the skills of power and empowerment? What good is it to study the racism suffered if the ways of resistance through the written word, research, voice, and collective action are not only studied, but learned and learned well? —Brian Gibbs

Before Brian began his teaching career, he always knew that teaching in a public school would have constraints. There were particular things you were supposed to teach and there would always be a standardized exam somewhere near the end. He fantasized about schools, which he thought of as mostly private ones, where teachers would take their students into the "educational wilds." These schools would educate the students as creatively and powerfully as possible, help them find themselves, and grow and prepare them for themselves, their community, and the world beyond. Additionally, they would help them recognize their own power and their own possibilities, help them to *become*.

When he was tasked with teaching world history first, which was a survey course mostly focused on Western civilization rather than the whole world, the course outline of mandated content jumped from country and continent with abandon. It travelled through time chronologically, in order but with no real connectivity or understanding. Nothing that allowed for comparison, deep analysis, or ability to connect content to the present; there was no real way to use the history other than as a body of content that is to be learned, absorbed, and "multiple choiced." There was no way to get at the deeper wisdom that could be revealed. This was his second year of teaching, and it was about this time that he read the *History-Social Science Framework for California Public Schools* from cover to cover several times. He noticed that nowhere in its 232 pages did it say that the content needs to be taught in any particular order or in any particular way. This is when he became as he puts it, a "jailhouse lawyer."

Brian read everything that the district used that might impact his teaching so he could critique it and counter it, and offer an alternative interpretation. He also began subscribing to *Rethinking Schools, Phi Delta Kappan, Radical Teacher, Teachers College Record,* and *Harvard Educational Review* among other journals to better defend what he was beginning to do. Once he realized that he didn't have to teach Chapter 1, Chapter 2, and Chapter 3 in a chronological death march, he began to think about how he might connect information and ideas together *thematically* and provocatively so they would set both his students and himself free. This is when he stumbled on "essential questions."

HOW DO YOU DEAL WITH MANDATED CONTENT?

Brian, Laura, and Jared: "We craft essential questions"

According to Ted Sizer and the work of the Coalition of Essential Schools (Sizer, 1992), essential questions are supposed to be powerful, justice oriented, nonbinary, difficult to answer, have mutual and competing answers, provocative, beg to be answered, and are a way to connect to students' current existence. A number of our veteran teachers, including Laura and Jared, were in agreement, both in this definition and in their importance. In Brian's view, the trouble with essential questions today is that they have become ubiquitous and misused. The trouble with school "reform" is that it takes radical pedagogical approaches like essential questions and knocks their teeth out. Powerful essential questions like, *What does it mean to be free?, How do we emancipate ourselves?, How do we create equality?,* and *How do we heal?,* get replaced in schools by nonessential questions like *Why did the first peoples come to the Americas?* A question that can be looked up in any textbook, online, or in an encyclopedia and demands no application, analysis, synthesis, or critical thought at all.

Essential questions that were either created by Brian or borrowed from other teachers allowed him to thematically connect content. The focus on themes allowed his students time to delve deeper into content while at the same time analyzing and making connections between that content themselves. The first unit of the year-long 10th-grade world history course focused on government thinkers from the Enlightenment to the present day, a foundational unit to introduce different types of government using the essential question: *How should we rule?* The introduction given by this unit was deepened and expanded on by each following unit. The second unit focused on the French Revolution from 1785–1815 driven by the question, *How do we stop the cycle of revolution?*, followed by the Russian Revolution 1917–1954 with the essential questions, *What does it mean to be equal?, How do we create equality?*, the Mexican Independence and Revolution 1810–1934 with the essential questions, *What is a hero?, What is a good leader?*, and the semester ending Chinese Revolution 1895–1965 with the semester encompassing question, *How do we have a successful revolution?* Set free from a specific chronology, students examine a topic in-depth analyzing choice and action, alternatives, and are driven by a compelling question that easily connects also to themselves and their lived experiences. Students analyze the structure of their families, their neighborhoods, their schools, and their classrooms. Students wrestle with what needs to be changed in their lives, neighborhoods, and schools. They then analyze the myriad ways in which change has been envisioned and attempted in the past to determine what might work currently and in the future. Last, students wrestle with change across time and examined individuals, both well known and little known involved in the decisions to make change.

For her Identity and Relevance Today unit in the RCGS course, Laura developed a set of guiding essential questions as well:

- What issues and philosophies separate conservatives and progressives?
- What are different explanations given for the existence of poverty or social class?
- Is there social mobility in the United States?
- How does class intersect with gender and race?
- How does the criminal justice system privilege the wealthy?
- What are other unearned privileges of the wealthy?
- Overarching essential question: Can there be justice and equality of opportunity within a capitalist system?

And Jared, for his Native American unit to be described next and in the following chapter, did the same:

- Did the White man bring civilization, or destroy it?
- What are the best ways to preserve life? Culture?
- What choices did Native American leaders have in the face of U.S. expansion?

- Sub-question: What kinds of things did Americans believe in that made it possible for the near-extermination of an entire population of people?
- A final Free Response Question (FRQ) writing task using documents: Was Native American removal genocide?

For Brian, Laura, Jared, and many of the other teachers in this study, essential questions served as means for them to teach thematically and deeply. In using essential questions to guide their teaching, they were better able to frame student inquiry and promote critical thinking in their classrooms.

Jared: "I dig a posthole where standards don't"

Another approach for dealing with mandated content, as advocated by our teachers and the research, is to "dig a posthole" into a standard that doesn't usually get too much attention (Virtue, Buchanan, & Vogler, 2012). "Digging a posthole" means if you have 86 line items in your content standards for that course, you identify a smaller number of those standards that you feel would merit a longer amount of attention and depth. You may more briefly "cover" those other standards, but would slow down considerably around the ones you have chosen. For example, framed by the essential questions listed above, Jared began developing a Native American History unit in his second year of teaching 11th-grade U.S. history to exist as a stand-alone unit, rather than as an added piece to a larger unit on expansionism and imperialism during the 1800s. This unit focused on—or dug a posthole in—the five (of 86) 8th-grade standards where Native Americans were either fully or partially the focus. This unit was very much inspired by and borrows from the work of his methods teacher, who also happens to be Brian.

As a passionate student of Native American studies in college and beyond, Jared wanted to "do justice" to these histories, and provide students the depth and complexity of this history that only a dedicated unit can achieve. Because of the depth of the content of this unit, it requires a fairly long amount of time, somewhere between 5 and 7 weeks depending on the version. In Jared's experience, students never get bored with this content, they always remember this history, and their most passionate feelings emerge out of this unit.

Over time, the unit has undergone constant rethinking, revision, and reworking. It has been overhauled multiple times. It has been researched thoroughly. And, Jared admits, it still has a long way to go. It still needs content upgrades, more options for assessment, and more region-specific Native American histories. One major weakness is the lack of women's history in this unit. This last year, a few of his students chose to research topics relating to Native American women's leadership roles in pre- and post-Columbian America, so he is hopeful that this previously missing content can be added, thanks to his students.

Additionally, Jared states that the intent of the unit is not to apologize or make justifications for the colonizing and mass removal of Native Americans. It is also not to eulogize or create sympathy for Native Americans. The purpose is to *deepen* and *complicate* students' thinking about the history of Native Americans, and to humanize this history as much as possible. Jared feels that teachers must get their students to conduct a critical examination of how the United States came to be the way it is today—not via a mixing in of stories here and there—but by flipping the perspective to a completely indigenous viewpoint of the last 600 some-odd years of American history. Jared argues that by doing this teachers can fulfill a major goal of justice-oriented education: To learn alternate histories of marginalized peoples in order to empower students to critically deal with current societal problems and oppressions. If he took the egregiously small amount of time suggested by the number of either the 8th-grade or 11th-grade California content standards that explicitly mentioned Native Americans and other marginalized groups, he would not be able to fulfill this important goal.

CONCLUSION

In this chapter, we saw how our letter writers and three veteran focus teachers select, emphasize, de-emphasize, and organize content, in both information and format, to achieve their goals of a justice-oriented curriculum in a standards-based, CCSS-focused classroom. Clearly, one of the pieces of content that all of them wish to teach their students is a skill-related one: that of critical literacy. All three focus teachers offered multiple opportunities for students to review, analyze, compare, and contrast multiple perspectives represented by multiple texts, while also keeping a focus on including those sources and stories that have been marginalized in the telling of history.

This critical literacy is with a purpose: to keep students at the center, to have them understand the power of their own knowledge and stories, and to create their own solutions. In so doing, using this content these teachers hope to create the kind of "critical hope"

(Duncan-Andrade, 2009) that occurs when (1) students are given the sense of control young people have when they are given the resources to deal with the forces that affect their lives, (2) both teachers and students painfully examine their lives and actions within an unjust society and share the sensibility that pain may pave the path to justice, and (3) stand in solidarity with one another and against self-interest and oppression. Pedagogically, as we will see in the next chapter, the goals are much the same.

CHAPTER 5

Students Have the Answers

Pedagogies of Possibility and Power

> Social change must be reflective and responsive to the community that is seeking justice. Schools, as part of a community, encompass the personalities, histories, conflicts, and celebrations of many more people than just those in the school building in the course of one year. Our mission is to know what is best for the young people in front of us; to do this we must know about their broader world and we cannot act as if this understanding can be achieved quickly. For us, as teachers, to be effective agents of change we must become familiar with all of these interlocking parts.
>
> —Amelie Baker

In teacher education, much is made, and rightfully so, of the need to encourage new teachers to develop their own "voice"; one unique to them, to their strengths, and to their passions. In short, to "teach who they are." This encouragement though may unintentionally leave out another very important individual in the teaching and learning process: the student. In a justice-oriented social studies classroom, as teachers look back into the past to figure out what/how to teach, they must also pay very close pedagogical attention to the young people right there in front of them (or around them depending on the classroom setup). In Chapter 4, our veteran teachers shared how they pay this type of attention in terms of the content they choose, but what does it look like pedagogically? In the chapter that follows, we will examine the diversity of teachers' justice-oriented *pedagogical* approaches in engaging with their students and with content, with an emphasis on their efforts to reconceptualize power and agency in standards-aligned social studies classrooms. Similar to Chapter 4, we will cite examples from our veteran teachers' classrooms and curricula, just Brian and Jared this time, to illustrate content-driven strategies for teaching to social justice topics and themes in history and contemporary society.

RELATIONSHIPS, TRUST, AND STUDENT KNOWLEDGE

On the topic of justice-oriented pedagogy, what many of our veteran teachers noted as an important aspect of how they taught, and indeed why they taught, was to get to know their students well. Our teachers wanted to be responsive to their students' needs; to develop close, trusting relationships with them and their families; and to nurture supportive and collegial relationships between their students. Additionally, as we saw in the previous chapters, they wanted to know what their students were interested in, and what they thought about and did on a daily basis. As Jennifer Shah advised new teachers,

> Get to know your students' cultures and interests outside of school. Know what is currently trending in their world and integrate that knowledge into lessons but allow students to take the lead. Issues in the 21st century include gangs, guns, immigration, poverty, inequity in education, and intolerance. The citizens of the world that sit in your classrooms right now will be the ones tackling these issues as the next lawmakers, educators, and activists. As their social studies educator what will you contribute to their journey and development? What kind of change do you want to see in our world in the next 20 years?

These goals fall in line with two of Wade's (2001) elements of a social justice education: that it is *student-centered* and *multicultural*. In order to share ideas openly and collaborate on issues of mutual concern, students need to feel cared for and respected to learn to trust one another. In order to achieve this, teachers need to respect students' abilities, interests, and opinions, and encourage students to make connections between themselves and the curriculum (Cushman, 2005). Additionally, teachers must be culturally knowledgeable, seeking out advice from colleagues, parents, and community members for working most effectively with all of their students.

THE CENTRALITY OF DIALOGUE AND ENGAGEMENT

A second key theme in the responses of our veteran teachers was the need to create multiple spaces and opportunities for dialogue in their classroom: structured and unstructured, teacher-led and student-led. They felt it important to support students in the development of their own voice, and to learn how to listen with an open mind and heart to voices that were not their own. As Eran DeSilva put it,

> Consider how different the current debate on immigration would be if our nation's leaders *truly* listened to other leaders or community members in the Western Hemisphere. What if elected officials listened to a wide array of voices before reacting to national crisis at our borders? Perhaps we would have more thoughtful and just policies. The next generation of leaders and voters can begin to genuinely listen with care to various perspectives before making critical decisions that will impact their community.

Once this *collaborative* classroom community was established, they could then fully engage with their students through the use of more *experiential* forms of teaching and learning history and social studies. According to Wade (2001) and our teachers, student involvement and engagement in mentally and physically active experiences are essential in the justice-oriented classroom. Through projects, role-playing, mock trials, simulations, and experiments, students experience concepts and key ideas firsthand, rather than just reading or hearing about them.

TAKING ACTION IN THE WORLD

According to Nieto (2000), truly multicultural education requires a commitment to both content and process. As part of their work, social justice educators collect information, ask critical questions of that information, and take action based on that critique in the interest of moving toward social justice. For our veteran teachers, regardless of how much their students "learned" in their classroom as far as knowledge and skills, if they didn't end up taking action with it, their job wasn't done. According to them, along with learning about social problems and questioning prevailing practices, they had to create opportunities for their students to work for social change. In particular, social justice teachers encourage students to work for the rights of those who are dominated or marginalized, through the creation of student-led activist clubs, through action research projects that focused on issues in their community and across the globe and possible solutions (Rubin,

2011), and through well-crafted service learning opportunities. Eran shares her advice with us again:

> Influential activists such as Gandhi, Malcolm X, and Eleanor Roosevelt were innovative thinkers but also strong communicators who could inspire others. Educators can highlight these leaders' ability to mobilize and organize others to take action and demand reform. Students have an array of ways to communicate with others in this digital age—can we enable them to present their ideas thoughtfully and effectively? If so, they can help empower others to be agents of change as well, building a social justice movement.

In the remaining sections of this chapter, please consider how, in Brian's unit examples from his world and U.S. history courses and in Jared's Native American History unit, both focus teachers develop the relationships and trust necessary to regularly engage all of their students in dialogue and experiencing history, and provide opportunities for them to take justice-oriented action as a result.

LIVING HISTORY

Brian's teaching is attentive to many goals of the CCSS, as he wants his students to read a lot and from multiple genres, write for different audiences in different genres, learn to plan arguments and questions, learn to think on their feet in the moment, take on a critical perspective, be able to offer thoughtful critiques, translate their arguments into art, and work together successfully as a team. But he also wants his students to get as close to the history as possible and to gain wisdom from it. Much like Laura and her RCGS course, he wants students to see the connectivity between race, class, gender, and sexual orientation, how oppressive the world and people can be, and how people have also always fought back, with the understanding that there are often only partial victories and how to keep cynicism at bay. Because Brian wants his students to become justice- and activist-oriented, he focuses on the intellectual skills he feels are necessary for change: self-reflection, teamwork, use of voice, making and defending arguments, analysis, synthesis, application, independence of mind, and inquiry among others. Students are assessed through structures like Socratic Seminar, character-driven seminar, experientials, simulations, and many other ways.

Living Structures: Socratic Seminars, Character-Driven Seminars, Experientials, and Simulations

According to Brian, a *Socratic Seminar* is "a ritualized intellectual discussion that centers on the powerful, often philosophical or moral ideas embedded within a text." A text can be anything that is rigorous, rich, has multiple viewpoints, and is connected to what is being learned or explored in class. Texts can include but are not limited to essays, poems, short stories, chapters from a novel, photographs, paintings, sculpture, plays, and so on. Socratic Seminars are typically facilitated by a teacher, but are very much student-led and driven. A *character-driven seminar* is an essential question-driven discussion that is run by seminar rules in which students are assigned a point of view, usually a historical figure. The purpose of the discussion is for students to argue about the essential question from a particular point of view. The end of the discussion is not preordained by actual history; rather, it is a discussion about history, point of view, and content, but not a reliving of it. An *experiential* is a content delivery system in which students reenact an historical event. Experientials are facilitated by a teacher and no previous content or understanding is needed to have students engage in an experiential. In short, history is "done to them." A *historical simulation/role-play* involves a student reenactment/discussion of an historical event using assigned roles. The outcome of the event is preordained by actual historical events. In the descriptions of the units that follow, you will see examples of these important and highly effective structures.

The French Revolution Unit

In the case of Brian's unit on the French Revolution as part of a 10th-grade world history course, students arrive on the first day unsure what is going to happen. He asks them to empty their backpacks and pockets of everything except things that are illegal. They have to sell everything as if at a garage sale, and only things they own and have with them—no textbooks, or houses that are owned by their parents. Based on the amount that they have left, they are assigned a role: king for the male student with the most, queen for the female student with the most, the next four are clergy, and the next seven are nobles. The point is for students to understand how people are born into circumstances beyond their control.

Students then go home and read several documents and come back to an experiential or reenactment of the years 1785–1789. By the end, the students who are king and queen understand how trapped they were in the legal process and trappings of royalty, and the peasants understand how unfair the system is and how trapped they are in it. The next day, students arrive and as the same broad characters they experience the arguments of the Estates General. The nobles and clergy each get one vote—for their small size—while the peasants get one vote only for their incredibly large size. The peasants as the 3rd Estate revolt, signing the Declaration of the Rights of Man and Citizen. They reflect on the events of the day, and for homework we then analyze the text of the Declaration in seminar.

Students choose to "become" different historical figures for the rest of the Revolution. Students analyze the Declaration to see if it does what their character wants and what the 3rd Estate wanted. They then experience the new government and the changes to France as their characters—wearing self-created nametags. This includes the creation of the "Republic," the National Assembly and the trial and execution of the king, the Reign of Terror, the rise of Napoleon, and the new king. Students make arguments, develop questions, and engage in several different character-driven seminars. For these seminars, students analyze the character descriptions, which include thick descriptions of character points of view, life choices, life experiences, and details of the time. The character descriptions that Brian provides for them reveal and teach much about the lives of the characters and the historical time period. The descriptions stay away from making arguments or pronouncements and instead provide detail and ambiguity. When it's over, students examine what went wrong, what went right, how the 3rd Estate could have gotten what was needed, and how this revolution, its characters, and its events might inform our choice for change in our current lives, school, neighborhood, city, country, and world.

Wars and Justice

For Brian's U.S. history course students he begins with a unit on war driven by the essential questions, *What is a just war?* and *How do we end war?* As the United States has been a country at war for some time now, Brian feels it is important to examine the historical antecedents of our country's participation in war and use it to better understand and shift and/or end our current predicament. The unit begins by asking students for what reasons would they themselves go to war or send someone they love to war? Students discuss the responses in small teams, as a whole class, and then complicate them:

What if we were invaded?
What if an ally requested our assistance?

What if a country was mistreating a minority population?
What if they were murdering them?
What if women were treated as second-class citizens?
What if a country was invading and taking over economically or militarily weaker countries that were not our allies?
What if another country was gathering control of resources that our country needed?

Next, students are asked to apply their definitions to secondary and primary descriptions of each of U.S. wars' beginnings, from the American Revolution through our current wars in Iraq and Afghanistan. Taking each in turn, students analyze the texts listing what reasons are justified for beginning the war and which are not, which usually leads to lots of discussion and argument. When this is completed, students are then asked to sort the wars into order from the most to the least "just," or the most just reasons for going to war to the least just reasons for going to war. Students then write reasons for why they were in that order. Students share their answers in teams, and then it becomes a whole-class discussion/argument. Students usually have strong reactions and arguments—which include some students arguing that there are *no* just reasons for any of America's wars. Other students argue that there is no just reason but that some wars were "necessary," and many other students are unsure what they think. The first time Brian taught the unit, the class voted on which war was the "most just," and began a 16-year tie between the Civil War and WWII.

WWII and Vietnam as Case Studies of Injustice

Knowing that students will have studied WWII in the previous year's world history course, Brian focuses their study on some of the lesser studied elements of WWII:

- Executive Order 9066 and the internment of Japanese and Japanese Americans
- military tactics used during the war, including area bombing, and the decision to not purposely liberate Nazi concentration and extermination camps
- the racism and sexism against, and undercelebration of, female, Native American, and African American troops, among others
- the inhumane treatment of prisoners
- the dropping of the atomic bomb and whether it was necessary, in order to deeply examine the often-argued "most justified war."

When their examination is completed, students engage in a wide-ranging Socratic Seminar using multiple texts, and then write a large essay explaining their own definition of a just war.

Brian's students then transition to the next case study, what students usually consider to be the "most unjust war": Vietnam. The class compares choices and experiences in Vietnam to those in WWII to challenge our notion of a just war, and examine how to end an unjust war, or a just war for that matter. Students examine how the war began, how it was fought, the average age of the soldiers, the tactics used, the leaders that were involved, the life of an ordinary soldier (both American and Vietnamese), the My Lai Massacre, particular battles, and particular presidential decisions.

The unit then examines the antiwar movements that began in the mid-1960s, including the Students for a Democratic Society (SDS), Youth International Party (Yippies), Weather Underground, Vietnam Veterans Against War (VVAW), the Berrigan brothers (Daniel and Phillip Berrigan), and Daniel Ellsberg. Students divide into teams, are assigned a character, read secondary and primary sources on their character, determine what the character's point of view on the war and all war is, and how the war should be ended. Students develop character analyses for their own character by writing in the first person, and for the other characters by writing them in third person. Each student develops a testimony explaining who they are, why they should be listened to, how the war should be ended, and why their perspective is the best one. In teams, students also develop high-level questions challenging the characters whose points of view are in opposition to theirs.

On seminar day, students one at a time deliver their testimony in the center of the classroom circle, to the applause of all. Once this is completed, the seminar commences. All teams argue their point of view about the best way to end the war in Vietnam particularly, and all wars in general. Three students are asked to remain "unconvinced," and they listen to the arguments, asking questions, making arguments, and in the end they decide who they think "won" the seminar. This character-driven seminar is generally a 2-day process, with testimonies and the beginning of the seminar on the first day, with the full day of seminar on the second day.

DEALING WITH PAINFUL TRUTHS

Inspired and drawn from Brian's teaching practice, and then developed for his school context, Jared's Native American History unit has two distinct parts that work chronologically within the frameworks of race and Native American experiences. It is a unit dedicated to Native American history, and also to the *inverse* teaching approach of major U.S. topics that often only get analyzed from a White, male, and patriotic perspective.

The first part of this unit is a survey of Native American history in the United States, centered on the essential question: *Did the White man bring civilization to the Americas, or did they destroy it?* Students start by studying the peopling and lifeways of the original inhabitants of the Americas prior to European arrival. Then they look at the invasions of the Spanish, French, and British, and how they used different tactics to divide, subdue, and push out indigenous peoples. They study the collisions of cultures and their disastrous effects on the people of the Americas from the arrival of Columbus all the way to the forming of the United States. In terms of resources, students read excerpts from many books to learn this history, including *Lies My Teacher Told Me, A People's History of the United States, Bury My Heart at Wounded Knee, A Different Mirror,* and *California*. Students also analyze and question commonly perpetuated myths regarding Native Americans, including the use of the term "civilized," the story of Thanksgiving, the reactions of the Pueblo toward Spanish forced cultural and religious reeducation, the California mission system, and the Gold Rush and its effects on Native Americans.

The second part of the unit focuses on Native American responses to U.S. expansion and centers around the questions: *What are the best ways to preserve life? Culture? And what choices did Native American leaders have in the face of U.S. expansion?* This part launches right off the first part by introducing how the United States utilized the belief that it had the "God-given right" to justify expansion of its borders across the Western Hemisphere. Ideas of race "science" and accepted social stratifications created an ideology of superiority of U.S. political leaders that fueled an aggressive policy toward land acquisition. Starting with bought land and moving toward taken land and broken treaties, students explore how the United States aggressively expanded its borders during the 19th century. They trace the westward movement through the Deep South, the borderlands, the West, and the North also in the context of industrialization and imperialism. In doing so, students study the lived experiences of the Seminole, Creek, Cherokee, Pueblo, Apache, and Sioux. In terms of resources, they analyze a wealth of speeches and letters written from Black Elk to Speckled Snake, and from John Ross to Chief Joseph. More in-depth studies are done, particularly on the Sioux, led by Red Cloud. The biography of Red Cloud, *The Heart of Everything That Is,* is an excellent source for this material.

The culminating part of the unit is when students are assigned roles of various leaders to represent at a simulated frozen-in-time meeting: a character-driven seminar. Leaders such as Tecumseh, Standing Bear, Cochise, Sitting Bull, Captain Jack, and Little Crow are brought to life in this conference, to discuss what they are going through and what decisions rest on their shoulders. For this part, Jared used to focus mainly on instances of resistance against White expansion. As Jared wanted students to view this history with more choices and nuance than that structure allowed, his students instead collect and analyze the stories that include a variety of perspectives from many different leaders with philosophies covering the spectrum of acceptance, escape, revolt, assimilation, and syncretism. The primary goal is to complicate students' thinking around responding to aggression when the main concerns are protecting the lives and cultures of one's people.

Jared has found student engagement in the character-driven speech and seminar portions to be sky-high when they are confronted with a challenging situation that has no apparent solution. Previously, it was too easy to say "We should fight back!" when speaking hypothetically. But after doing in-depth, careful, personal studies of these leaders, the students tend to grow very attached to them, and want to do right by them. Their dialogue with one another is always rich and deeply moving. It's a serious historical topic, and the students get that.

After this project, Jared's classes take a day to look at the eventual fates of the leaders and their tribes. Students then conduct document studies to put together the story of the Wounded Knee Massacre. The unit concludes with document studies and listening to interviews with prominent contemporary Native American leaders to understand the present Native American reservation system and recent struggles and victories of these communities today, with a push for students to concretely think about how they might act to make these situations better in the future.

CONCLUSION

In this chapter, we shared justice-oriented pedagogies from Brian and Jared's classrooms. Both Brian and Jared focused on creating opportunities for students to engage with content and with each other;

students are clearly at the center of their activities. To experience and indeed *live* history is essential to students connecting emotionally, physically, and intellectually with the stories of the past. By doing this, they can then begin to connect the lives of people who came before them with their own lives and those they love and care for. This way, when students see something happening in their community, in the classroom, in their country, or in the world that they feel to be unjust or unfair, they are more likely to act. They will make the choice to *not* be a bystander, and instead will stand up for what they believe in. In these justice-oriented social studies classrooms, students will have already connected emotionally and physically to the experiences of those who have made one or both of these choices, and they will know what is possible: a better, more socially just world. And that they have the power to make it that way.

Part III

WITHIN AND BEYOND THE CLASSROOM: JUSTICE-ORIENTED AGENCY AND ACTIVISM

Learning to teach for social justice is an act of becoming. Regardless of how well prepared we think we are, we are invariably challenged and stretched by our curriculum, our context, and our students. Many justice-oriented teachers describe their journey as a series of transformations, in which they had to reimagine themselves in response to the tensions and challenges of teaching in a system that prioritizes accountability over justice. In the next three chapters, we focus on the iterative process of learning to teach for social justice. In Chapter 6, we examine how teachers learn to teach for social justice, using the teachers' stories to illustrate how they develop and learn to enact their social justice vision. Chapter 7 explores the challenges faced by justice-oriented teachers, overall and specifically within the field of social studies, as they reconcile the demands of teaching toward their conscience in an accountability-driven classroom. We highlight teachers' advice regarding how they overcame these challenges, with a focus on how we can draw on mentors and the professional community as a strategy for sustaining and supporting our work. Finally, in Chapter 8, we grapple with the political implications of teaching for social justice, as we examine strategies for reclaiming agency and reconceptualizing "accountability" as justice-oriented teachers. Throughout, we include resources for teachers interested in finding ways to enact justice within and beyond the classroom.

CHAPTER 6

Becoming a Renegade

Preparing to Teach for Social Justice

Dear Teacher,
May you be a revolutionary hopefully, but a renegade absolutely.

—Brian Gibbs

BECOMING A SOCIAL JUSTICE TEACHER

During Back-to-School night, I often candidly tell parents, "In my final quarter of college, I was freaking out about getting a job . . . so I decided to teach." Of course, parents then look at me bewildered as they think to themselves, "Why would you ever say that out loud?" (I secretly like this stunned reaction because now I have an attentive class.) I quickly explain the reason I chose teaching was not quite so capricious. I entered education because I had a thirst for social justice and believed that education is a critical step in realizing a more just world. Education empowers people to think and analyze issues so that they can make thoughtful choices that can bring about peace, justice, and equity. This introduction on Back-to-School night helps parents understand what motivates me to teach social studies to their teenagers.

Though I had great intentions as I began teaching, I soon realized that I was not going to be the next Erin Gruwell (*Freedom Writers*) or John Keating *(Dead Poets Society)*. Not only were these iconic pop culture figures an unrealistic expectation for a new educator, but also teaching required more than just good intentions and grit. It required skill, a strong work ethic, expertise, stamina, practice, and studying. Moreover, it required knowledge of sound pedagogy, standards, and expectations of teachers set forth by my school and government.

—Eran DeSilva

Like Eran, many of us enter the field with grand visions. We imagine our future classrooms characterized by vibrant discussions about critically important issues of justice. We see ourselves as engaging, energetic, and creative facilitators, fostering student-led and academically rigorous investigations of historical, contemporary, and disciplinary questions. We imagine doing this on a daily basis, drawing on our rich relationships with students, robust collegial relationships, and limitless curricular resources. In reality, however, learning to teach—both overall, and for social justice specifically—is a complex endeavor (Agarwal, 2011). In addition to the curricular and pedagogical expertise characteristic of all good teachers, teaching for social justice also requires us to be reflective and reflexive as we respond to local and global issues of inequity and justice. We have to gain fluency in our students' worlds and communities, learn to advocate for ourselves and our stance, and negotiate an ever-increasing array of mandates. Eran is right: Teaching is hard.

Thankfully, however, we don't have to engage in this work alone. Justice-oriented teachers can rely on the examples of educators and activists that came before them, connect with supportive colleagues, and work collectively to define and enact their vision in the classroom. In the next section, we look at some of the ways teachers prepare for the philosophical, political, and practical demands of teaching for social justice.

EXAMINE YOUR STANCE

In Chapter 2 we described three different stances that teachers can take when enacting justice in highly regulated contexts. Teachers can embrace educational policies that align with or facilitate their vision. For some of the teachers in this book, the widespread adoption of the Common Core State Standards (CCSS) brings curricular flexibility and a validation of their efforts to center critical literacy. Eran and Laura, whom we met in Chapter 1, welcome the CCSS's emphasis on critical thinking as a window into justice-oriented curriculum. Teachers can also take advantage of curricular reform as an opportunity to redefine their field. In Chapter 2, we examined how Brian draws on this perspective when he encourages teachers to use the standards to recenter equity and justice as they shape the future of social studies. By working in solidarity with colleagues, Brian used the CCSS to advocate for justice-oriented curricular transformation in their district, thus reclaiming agency in the face of efforts toward standardization. And teachers can resist, especially by refusing to allow external mandates to undermine their professional autonomy and curricular emphases. Michael conjures this stance in his letter, as he urges teachers to stand up, push back, and opt out of unjust mandates.

These are all valid approaches to responding to the CCSS and related accountability mandates, especially when used as part of a broader effort to promote social justice in curriculum, policy, and schooling writ large. Enacting justice is a complex and multifaceted endeavor, and requires teachers to use the strategies best suited to their vision and local context. However, one's stance is not value-neutral. Teaching is an inherently political act, and the vision that we bring to our work informs each decision we make in the classroom. While most justice-oriented teachers will invariably embrace, reframe, and resist aspects of the CCSS—and most other education reforms—it is imperative that we consider how our decisions impact our students and a broader vision of justice.

Each of us has seen a range of approaches to social justice among our students and fellow teachers. In Alison's research on justice-oriented approaches to English language arts, for example, she examined how teachers' social justice philosophies and school contexts affect their curricular, philosophical, and activist priorities (Dover, 2015). After analyzing 24 teachers' approaches to using standards-aligned curriculum to address a broad range of social justice concepts and literacy-related skills, she found that teachers' emphasis on *either* using social justice content to promote students' English language arts learning, *or* using English language arts content to promote students social justice learnings, had profound curricular and pedagogical implications. Two of the teachers in her study, for example, created justice-oriented curricular units related to Elie Wiesel's Holocaust memoir, *Night* (Wiesel & Wiesel, 2006). Both used *Night* as a foundation for addressing specific English language arts content standards, examining the social and historical context of the Holocaust, and analyzing contemporary examples of oppression; however, they had dramatically different classroom-level emphases. For one teacher, whose vision of teaching for social justice centralized raising awareness and promoting acceptance, teaching *Night* was an opportunity to use a justice-oriented text to examine students' experiences with prejudice and inequity. For the other, who framed teaching for social justice as a step toward social reconstruction, it was the springboard for a comprehensive analysis of racially motivated genocide in contemporary society. (See Dover, 2015, for a detailed analysis of these units.)

Similar trends are visible throughout the literature on teaching for social justice. Picower (2012), for example, examines the relationship between social justice teaching inside the classroom and in the broader community, ultimately concluding that justice-oriented teachers must situate their efforts within a broader agenda of social action. She challenges teachers to make three commitments to increase their impact: to envision a socially just world and work to reconcile their vision with the realities of inequity; to move toward liberation by getting students to be conscious, active participants in the world; and to stand up to oppression by engaging in ongoing and collective action in response to school- and community-based injustice (pp. 87–88).

Westheimer and Kahne's (2004) analysis of justice-oriented approaches to democratic education offers a valuable lens for considering the impact of teacher vision. Based on their analysis of two years of qualitative and quantitative data regarding high school civic education programs (including observations, interviews, and pre- and postsurveys), they developed a conceptual framework depicting philosophies of citizenship as personally responsible, participatory, or justice-oriented. In addition to citing different programmatic emphases, they found that "successful" democratic education programs can "promote very different outcomes [a]nd these differences often are politically significant" (p. 20). Students in programs that emphasized participatory citizenship developed different skills and values (e.g., a vision of themselves as community leaders) than those in justice-oriented programs (e.g., an interest in politics and social activism). Just as democratic educators' visions impact what students learn about being a "good citizen," so, too, do our visions affect what our students learn about justice.

As you consider your own approach to teaching for social justice, we invite you to draw on the work of two social justice leaders, Carl Grant and Christine Sleeter, who invite teachers to articulate their visions of themselves as fantastic teachers (2011, p. 5). While most teacher preparation programs require candidates to reflect on their educational philosophy, we find this question especially effective for considering justice-oriented approaches to the CCSS and other educational dilemmas. We encourage you to ask yourself: What is your vision of yourself as a fantastic justice educator? What do you teach about? What does your classroom look, feel, and sound like? What kinds of pedagogy do you use? What do your students learn? How do you know? To whom are you accountable? How?

We also encourage you to consider how you hope to embody this vision within your classroom, your school, your local community, and the broader world. Do your efforts to enact social justice extend beyond the classroom? Why or why not? In what ways might you challenge yourself and your students to increase your impact? By engaging questions like these, and reflecting on them in moments of uncertainty, we have the opportunity to continue to teach toward our conscience throughout our careers. As Isabel, whom we met in Chapter 4, reminds us, "guided by vision [we are] able to navigate the revolving door of educational mandates, without ever allowing them to dictate [our] practice."

In the remainder of this chapter, we examine practical aspects of learning to teach for social justice, both before and during your first years in the classroom. However, regardless of where you are in your career, we encourage you to take advantage of every opportunity to reflect on your own vision and values, and what steps are necessary to translate them into classroom reality.

TAKE ADVANTAGE OF YOUR TEACHER EDUCATION PROGRAM

Many teacher education programs include social justice as one of their primary goals. In practice, however, justice-oriented teacher education programs are as varied as the candidates who enroll in them (Hytten & Bettez, 2011; Zeichner & Flessner, 2009). However, in other programs, "social justice" can be more of a slogan than a philosophy (Zeichner & Flessner, 2009), leading some to struggle to connect their preservice education to their efforts to teach for social justice. This difficulty is compounded by ongoing debates regarding the multiple meanings of social justice overall (see Chapter 1), and within teacher education specifically.

Beginning with the National Council for the Accreditation of Teacher Education's (NCATE) decision to eliminate the phrase "social justice" from its list of desirable dispositions among teacher candidates (Heybach, 2009; Powers, 2006), and continuing through current emphases on high-stakes, privatized teacher performance assessments like edTPA, teacher educators face intense political and practical pressure to standardize the definition of "good teaching." While much of this pressure reflects neoliberal emphases on individual, privatized interests rather than systemic responses to injustice (Picower, 2011), it also reflects a critical tension in the field of justice-oriented teacher education: that of preparing candidates—and their future students—to both succeed and enact justice within an extremely flawed, inequitable educational system.

Poplin and Rivera (2005) highlight the intensity of the challenge facing justice-oriented teacher educators when reflecting on how their own teacher education program prepared candidates. After being notified that their graduates would no longer be hired by a local, justice-oriented school district for failure to promote adequate academic progress, they had to reexamine their approach to preparing candidates to balance social critique and academic rigor. Ultimately, they came to embrace a vision of justice-oriented teacher education that centered both social justice and accountability by preparing candidates who are

> (a) aware of the critical racial–economic issues that influence schooling and multiple strategies for addressing these issues, (b) highly skilled in the content of the curriculum standards they are called to teach, (c) educated in multiple pedagogical theories and strategies that can be applied to the various content areas, (d) skilled in English language instruction, (e) able to assess their students' progress effectively, (f) able and committed to working alongside families and communities, and (g) inspired to develop strong commitments and effective attitudes necessary to raise achievement dramatically among the least privileged of their students. (p. 31)

We share this vision of preparing to teach for social justice as intrinsically connected to academically rigorous, contextually conscious practice. In the current context of accountability-driven reforms, this means that to be successful, justice-oriented teachers must be able to demonstrate their expertise in disciplinary content and skills, fluency in curricular standards and school-level requirements, and ability to promote student content-area learning. Simultaneously, learning to teach for social justice requires us to critique the very content areas, standards, and mandates to which we are attentive. The teachers in this book do this as they strategize about how to translate their social justice vision into social studies practice, shifting among stances of embracing, reframing, and resisting the CCSS according to their own beliefs and contextual reality.

Ideally, all candidates would attend preparation programs that challenge and prepare them to become justice-oriented, effective, and transformative teachers. Yet, we know that even the best programs are required to meet a growing number of state and federal mandates, creating tensions for candidates and teacher educators alike.

Teacher education programs—like schools themselves—are changing in response to national emphases on accountability, high-stakes assessment, and standardization.

Michael Swogger, a former teacher and current teacher educator at Penn State Harrisburg, describes the impact of these policies on justice-oriented teacher education:

> Hopefully, your teacher preparation program helped to instill an even greater sense of commitment to . . . the cause of social justice that so naturally coalesces with the subject matter you will teach. [However, there is] no doubt that same teacher preparation program was geared more and more to help you navigate teaching in the standards and high-stake testing era. I've seen this in my own experience as a social studies methods instructor just over the last six years. The emphasis in these programs has steadily shifted, from a balance between content and pedagogy to stressing aligning teaching, lesson plans, and assessments to state academic standards. And now, the vast majority of the states have adopted the *Common Core State Standards* to serve as the basis for all academic instruction, dictating to new teachers and their teacher education programs a new set of mandates around which their professional practice must revolve. I can imagine that perhaps you and teachers like you who are dedicated to teaching social justice feel more unsure of yourselves, as test-driven mandates like this are now the norm in American schooling.

Michael raises an important point regarding the contradictions inherent in learning to teach for social justice in a hostile educational climate. We encounter those tensions as teachers and teacher educators ourselves, leading us to adopt what Julie Gorlewski, a faculty member at SUNY New Paltz, has called "the dual stance of critical compliance and reflective resistance" (Gorlewski, 2015, p. 9). Grounded in critical pedagogy and Freirian concepts of "conscientization," this approach requires teachers and teacher educators to grapple with how to simultaneously learn to teach for social justice and prepare to meet state and federal mandates. By wrestling with the dilemmas associated with teaching for social justice in highly regulated preservice contexts, teachers can develop the skills necessary to enact justice in their own classrooms.

We model these approaches in our own classes. For example, in one of Alison's classes, pre- and inservice teachers research contextually relevant issues of justice, analyze justice-oriented curriculum for their discipline, and design original units that embody their vision of teaching for social justice. In addition to gaining experience with justice-oriented curriculum design, her students develop strategies for pitching their unit to administrators and community stakeholders, thus preparing them translate their vision into reality. (Additional information about this course, related activities, and sample assignments are available on her website at www.alisongdover.com.) Nick adopts a similar approach when he asks his students to examine data demonstrating the inequitable educational outcomes resulting from educational structures such as tracking and standardized tests, and participate in Socratic exercises to uncover the "common sense" ideology and beliefs that sustain these structures (Kumashiro, 2015). They then create lessons that might serve to resist and counter these ideologies and beliefs in their own classrooms and schools. In Ruchi's classroom, pre- and inservice teachers critically analyze CCSS and content state standards and then work to design a 5-day justice-oriented, literacy-based social studies lesson plan. Ruchi guides students through each facet of a framework she designed to help students restructure and reshape mandated curriculum: inspiring wonder, painting the picture, application, connecting the past to the present, and facilitating action (Agarwal-Rangnath, 2013). She enacts justice-oriented sample lessons in the classroom that highlight each tenet of the framework and then ends the lesson discussing with her students ways in which one can meet state and federal mandates, including integrating literacy into social studies content, and still teach social studies from a social justice perspective. (To learn more about the framework, see Ruchi's book, *Social Studies, Literacy, and Social Justice in the Common Core Classroom: A Guide for Teachers* [Agarwal-Rangnath, 2013].) These approaches are in line with those of many other justice-oriented teacher educators nationwide (e.g., Bieler, 2012; Murrell, 2001).

Some of the teachers in this book learned to teach in environments like these, that facilitated their growth as justice-oriented teachers. Jared, Tom, and David, for example, are all graduates of a program for which social justice was both a central focus and a critical outcome. As candidates in a social justice-oriented teacher education program, they (1) were recruited and trained as teacher candidates who demonstrate the most potential and drive to fight for educational equity and social justice (Haberman, 1995; Zeichner, 2003). Additionally, they were taught a curriculum that guided them in understanding and examining social inequalities, in becoming reflective educators knowledgeable in theories and practice of learning and teaching, and in taking action—individually and collectively—to remediate inequalities inside and outside the classroom (UCLA TEP, 2002). Then, they were placed in mostly under-resourced urban school settings for their student teaching and/or 1st-year teaching experiences, and the teacher education program developed long-term relationships with urban school districts and communities so that this was possible and productive (Murrell, 2001). Last, the program offered opportunities to participate in justice-oriented professional learning communities (PLCs) after graduation, to reflect on their practice and hold one another accountable for their development (see below for more on justice-oriented PLCs).

Other teachers, however, attended programs that placed less emphasis on social justice. Laura Einhorn, our focus teacher in Chapter 4, describes her experience as follows:

> My teacher preparation program was practical rather than theoretical, so I walked into the classroom on my first day ready to write the hell out of a backwards plan and assign detention slips without hesitation, but lacking a philosophical understanding of what it means to be a White, upper-class teacher in a school that serves mainly students of color from diverse economic backgrounds.

For Laura, much of her development as a social justice teacher has happened in the classroom itself:

> My process has been two-fold: to explore my own identity and privilege, and to educate myself in the history of the communities of the students I teach. It is an ongoing process and one I try to approach with humility and self-compassion. . . . Reach out to your community and your peers often and with humility. And be kind to yourself because this is a difficult and long process! I make mistakes often and my curriculum isn't good enough yet, but I am proud of my progress and my commitment to improving.

This idea of teaching for social justice as an ongoing, iterative process is shared by many justice-oriented teachers. When Jennifer Shah (whom you met in Chapter 1) struggled to teach for social justice during her first 2 years in the classroom, she returned to get a master's degree in a program that emphasized service learning. She learned a lot from her experience, and began to change her approach.

> During my first few years of teaching I would have my students participate in community service activities such as collecting donations or boxing at a food pantry. Disappointed with the lack of connection between the service and the curriculum, as well as [between] the students and the community, I tried something different. As part of a community asset-mapping project in graduate school, I had found a local shelter just blocks away. That year I integrated a service learning project with the unit on the Great Depression. At the time the United States was going through the worst recession since I was a child. After some scaffolding, my students made connections between what we were learning and the conditions of their own reality. More than that, they wanted to do something about it. My students were allowed with their permission to interview the residents at the shelter. After realizing that the residents depended on the food pantry, students wanted to go check it out. Upon investigation, they discovered that contents in the pantry violated the tenets of a healthy diet related to the food pyramid they learned about in science. When we returned to the classroom from our community fieldtrip, the students and I began brainstorming some solutions to the problem. We came up with hosting a food drive based on the food pyramid. We collected several well-balanced meals for the families at the shelter that year. Etched in my memory is a class of 12- and 13-year-olds all working together to help members of their community.

However, Jennifer, like many teachers, found that enacting justice-oriented teaching was more complicated than she anticipated. Despite her efforts to center questions of social justice, she continued to see deficit perspectives among her students.

> I was proud of my students and thought that this was teaching for social justice. I was mistaken. The students' reflective essays made it clear that they viewed the homeless as "the other" and developed what I now know as the savior complex believing that only they could solve the situation. The project and the discussions had not gone far enough. Through further action, reflection, and reading I continue to refine what it means to teach through the lens of social justice.

Jennifer's story highlights the ongoing, iterative nature of learning to teach for social justice—a theme that came up frequently in teachers' letters. Regardless of how justice-oriented our preservice education was, we have much to learn—from our students, our colleagues, and our community—as we continue our journey as social justice educators. Perhaps Dawn says it best when she encourages new teachers:

> Follow the lessons taught from the tortoise. Slow and steady wins the race. It is very difficult to challenge a system one is an integral part of. We can sometimes feel complicit in the inefficiency at best and oppression at worst when we cannot effect change. It can feel like operating in competing worlds. However, finding that balance between challenging and questioning and taking away what works for you, will keep you grounded in your pedagogy for a long career.

CONTINUE TO LEARN DURING YOUR FIRST YEARS

There are many benefits to attending a justice-oriented teacher preparation program. Justice-oriented teacher education can help you build community, meet mentors, and develop the curricular and pedagogical skills necessary to enact justice in a wide array of school settings. However, it is still just the beginning.

As we teach for and about social justice, we work to build curriculum that connects to our students' lives and prior learning. We challenge normative thought by integrating multiple perspectives into the curriculum, especially the voices of those dominated, marginalized, or traditionally excluded in texts. We find ways for students to connect the stories of struggle and resistance to contemporary social justice issues and make connections between historical events and present-day circumstances. We engage students in academically rigorous curriculum, having high expectations for all of our students. In addition, we work collaboratively with our students to make change in our school and community. This notion of social justice-oriented teaching is centered on the idea that social justice is about working toward, and about, meeting everyone's basic needs and fulfilling everyone's potential to live productive and empowering lives as participating citizens of our global community (Wade, 2007).

And yet, teaching social studies for social justice is not an easy endeavor. Even those preservice teachers who leave their social justice-oriented programs feeling prepared and committed to teach for social justice struggle to build, integrate, and enact social justice curriculum (Agarwal et al., 2010). Pressures and constraints, such as the pressure to raise test scores, may conflict with teachers' social justice leanings and require teachers committed to social justice to negotiate what they want to teach within the context of their individual school settings (Agarwal, 2011; Agarwal et al., 2010; Dover, 2013a).

In reflecting on her experience, Jennifer underscores the importance of taking advantage of the potential of justice-oriented preservice preparation, but also focusing on opportunities for continued growth.

> Continue to deconstruct and reconstruct your ideas about social justice on your own, through professional development, or by going back to school. If you choose to pursue a higher degree, be sure that the mission, vision, and values of the institution align with your own, especially related to social justice and its implementation out in the community. You can also create your own intentional professional learning communities and explore ideas with colleagues at your school or virtually anywhere in the world via social media.

As teachers are increasingly pressured to comply with accountability mandates, new teachers may struggle more than ever to figure out how to reconcile their social justice vision with the demands of the classroom. In the following chapter, we explore how justice-oriented teachers find mentors, build community, and engage in professional learning communities that support their growth.

CHAPTER 7

You Can Do This, but Not Alone

Build Community, Find Mentors, and Keep Your Job

Teaching is a high-stakes, high-impact profession, one that requires us to respond fluidly and flexibly to a stunning array of student, curricular, administrative, and community interests. Teachers have limited resources with which to purchase curricular, textual, and multimedia materials; less time than is necessary to effectively teach everything they would like to; and students with varied levels of interest in the content at hand. We are frequently underpaid, subject to widespread public speculation regarding our qualifications, and may or may not be part of a department that shares our commitment to social justice. As accountability mandates grow in number and prominence, teachers are increasingly asked to change their curriculum to accommodate technological and scheduling issues associated with high-stakes testing.

In this chapter, we examine some of the challenges faced by justice-oriented teachers, including institutional resistance, lack of resources, and external pressures toward standardization. We highlight teachers' advice regarding how they overcame these challenges, with a focus on the role of justice-oriented teacher communities and professional networks as a strategy for sustaining and supporting their work.

COMMON CHALLENGES FACED BY JUSTICE-ORIENTED TEACHERS

Beginning teachers face myriad challenges as they enter their first classrooms, including the growing emphasis on standards and accountability and lack of support or mentoring. In addition to these challenges, beginning teachers must learn how to manage their classroom, design and implement curriculum, organize desks, create assessments, prepare students for standardized tests, and so forth. Teachers are entering their classrooms with high hopes, and then questioning whether they've chosen the right profession. As teachers learn to untangle their role as an educator, and find ways to feel successful in the classroom, learning how to deal with the complexities and challenges surrounding their daily practice as teachers is especially important.

Current attrition rates for beginning teachers are high and continue to grow (van Hover & Yeager, 2004). Research on beginning teachers illustrates that novice teachers often struggle both psychologically and instructionally as they enter their first few years of teaching (van Hover & Yeager, 2004). Teachers feel frustrated with their lack of autonomy and inability to make decisions around key decisions that affect their role in the classroom (Kumashiro, 2015). With the increasing emphasis on high-stakes testing, standardized teacher performance assessments, and its impact on teacher autonomy, this frustration will likely grow (Au, 2013b). In addition, beginning teachers often are expected to assume all the same responsibilities as the more experienced teachers at their school (Bartell, 2004). Most beginning teachers receive little to no mentoring and support. Given these challenges, it is not uncommon for beginning teachers to feel exceptionally overwhelmed in their first few years.

Challenges for Beginning Social Studies Teachers

Novice social studies teachers must deal with the same foreseeable challenges as any beginning teacher, but are also faced with specific challenges related to content and instruction. "Best practices" that are often advocated in social studies research and in social studies methods, such as using primary and secondary sources to engage students in historical inquiry-based activities, are often a challenge for teachers to integrate into their first classroom. Inquiry-based activities may feel at odds with the mandated curriculum they are expected to teach. Additionally, social studies remains a multidisciplinary subject area that cover fields such as anthropology, archaeology, economics, geography, history, law, philosophy, political science, psychology, religion, and sociology. What and how to teach given the depth and breadth of content knowledge they must cover may feel extremely challenging to teachers.

Van Hover and Yeager (2004) engaged in a case study analysis of three secondary history teachers who graduated from the same teacher education program and are now in their second year of teaching. Their data revealed that each of the beginning teachers faced similar challenges regardless of their school setting. First, the new teachers were afraid of "losing control" of their students and thus focused on classroom management. Second, the teachers were concerned about covering content. Third, the teachers had doubt about their students' ability to think critically. Fourth, the teachers received little to no support in their first years of teaching. Amidst these challenges, the teachers chose lecture and textbooks over historical inquiry and other methods incorporating the "doing" of history that they had learned in their teacher education program.

Given the pressures social studies teachers face in regards to standardization and accountability, many teachers rely on their textbooks to manage challenges related to content coverage (Agarwal-Rangnath, 2013; van Hover & Yeager, 2004). Oftentimes administrations encourage social studies teachers to use textbooks to ensure students are receiving the content they need to be successful on standardized tests. However, teaching from the textbook directly, without encouraging students to question and critically think about the messages and assumptions embedded within these texts, may work to perpetuate a harmful storyline, which negates the experiences, voices, and presence of people whose acts of resistance and contributions have helped build the country we currently live in. As Johnson (2007) explains, traditional curriculum often "denies students the opportunity to benefit from the knowledge, perspectives, and understanding to be gained from studying other cultural groups' experiences and attaining the intercultural competency to work with everyone" (p. 146). By using primarily the textbook, students are severely limited in their understandings of historical content, as history is portrayed only from a single perspective.

With the Common Core in place, literacy is now a key component of all academic core classes. Social studies teachers will be expected to integrate literacy into their teaching, even as this may not be their area of expertise. Thieman and Leski (2015) argue that, "teachers need to have a grasp of discipline based literacy strategies to become proficient readers and consumers of social studies" (p. 14). Discipline-specific literacy strategies that students use in social studies include: building prior knowledge, building vocabulary, using knowledge of text structures and genres to predict main ideas, posing relevant questions, comparing claims across texts, and evaluating evidence (Thieman & Leski, 2015). As social studies teachers will be expected to emphasize literacy in their teaching, they will need to develop students ability to question, evaluate sources, use evidence to construct and present arguments and explanations, analyze problems, and take informed action (Thieman & Leski, 2015). Each of these facets of inquiry-based teaching encourage students to question and think about history, while simultaneously building students' literacy skills. For beginning teachers, learning to integrate the literacy strategies into their teaching may be challenging at first, but will help students to be strong, proficient readers, and thus students may be better able to examine and grapple with historical content. The struggle for many beginning social studies teachers will be learning how to integrate literacy into social studies content.

Challenges for Beginning Justice-Oriented Teachers

As a beginning teacher, one might struggle with the predictable pattern of challenges novices continue to face in the classroom, including classroom management and curriculum development (Bartell, 2004; Massey, 2004). Outside of learning the content they are expected to teach, beginning teachers will also need to learn how to build community with their students, organize their classroom, communicate with parents, create and implement assessments, and so forth. Learning to teach is a lifelong endeavor, where one needs time, nurturing, and support to develop their craft. For the case of justice-oriented teachers, this is especially important. Beginning social justice teachers are faced with an even more complex and dynamic learning curve. They must find space to teach social studies for social justice in today's context of standardization and accountability, which is especially challenging. Learning to manage curricular demands with one's vision for social justice education may be particularly daunting.

Beginning social studies teachers need to learn the content standards for their grade level, which may feel overwhelming and cumbersome in itself. Justice-oriented teachers need to learn the curriculum, and find resources outside of their textbook to help them create and enact social justice curriculum. For most beginning justice-oriented social studies teachers, learning how to implement large amounts of curriculum (Massey, 2004), while also understanding how to navigate a context of standardization and accountability to integrate social justice content (Flores, 2007; Johnson, Oppenheim, & Suh, 2009; Kelly & Brandes, 2001; Miller, Beliveau, DeStigter, Kirkland, & Rice, 2008; Sleeter, 2005), may feel especially complex. Teachers will need to learn how to implement the new standards, prepare students for high-stakes tests, and manage the daily challenges of teaching. Taking on these challenges, alongside the task of integrating social justice issues into the social studies curriculum, may feel unfeasible. As beginning teachers aim to translate their ideal into practice, their visions of social justice teaching may be complicated as they learn to manage and improvise curricular guidelines (Kauffman, Johnson, Kardos, Liu, & Peske, 2002; Kelly & Brandes, 2001) and navigate mandated curricular structures to enact justice-oriented curriculum (Sleeter, 2005).

The focus on standardization and testing in today's schools often leads to a narrowing of curriculum that excludes student interests, authentic instruction, and a thorough examination of critical social justice issues (Oakes & Lipton, 2003; Sleeter, 2005). Katy Swalwell, a social studies teacher educator at Iowa State University, echoes these findings in her letter. She claims that the "obsession with high-stakes testing . . . leads to a narrowing of the curriculum and a reduction of social studies instructional time." In other words, the pressure teachers face to prepare students for standardized tests may leave teachers to negotiate their curricular goals. Teachers may render their commitments to social justice as unfeasible or impossible, thus feeling forced to set aside their visions of social justice teaching to meet the demands of administration (Agarwal, 2011). Even as the CCSS allow for more flexibility and creativity, the high-stakes tests attached to the standards may determine changes to teachers' classrooms and curricular decisions.

As we discussed in Chapter 3, developing students' critical literacy is a key way of allowing our students to see the narratives of social injustice and inequality within texts. Justice-oriented teachers can be mindful of the messages and bias embedded within social studies textbooks and thus work intentionally to integrate the history and perspectives of all people. Teachers can juxtapose historical text and content against various points of reference and multiple perspectives, so that students may develop a more critical and comprehensive understanding of the past and present (Zinn, 2003). In social studies, multiple perspectives are used to analyze issues and ideas through the stories of those who may have been traditionally excluded in texts. The ability to understand multiple viewpoints may allow students to solve complex problems and become more globally aware of the complexity surrounding historical events. Integrating the history and perspectives of all people can be particularly challenging, as teachers often need to pull from outside resources to supplement and enrich the preexisting curriculum.

POLITICS OF TEACHING

According to the National Council for the Social Studies (NCSS), and the latest research in social studies education, social studies curriculum, instruction, and assessment at all grade levels continues to be marginalized, resulting in the reduction of instructional time and access to qualified social studies personnel and resources (Maguth, 2012). Given these obstacles and pressures, teaching social studies for social justice can be a particularly overwhelming and a complex endeavor for new educators. To teach for social justice requires one to not only breach a steep learning agenda, but to also navigate through a school context laden with challenges such as instructional pacing, meeting standards, test preparation, and adhering to a mandated curriculum.

Regardless, the marginalization of social studies and the lack of funding and investment given to the subject area is not the only challenge social studies teachers are up against. Katy Swalwell argues, "there are powerful forces at work shaping common sense around public schools, the problems to be fixed, and their solutions. We need to be aware of these forces, and be savvy as we try to navigate or influence them." Many of these challenges are rising as the first set of Common Core tests are being administered. Katy includes the following in the list of challenges teachers face here in the United States:

> The stripping of collective bargaining rights from teachers across the country that can reduce protections for teachers who address controversial issues in their classrooms, the continued tracking of students that reinforces economic and racial inequalities, discipline procedures that funnel students into a school-to-prison pipeline, the hyper-segregation of White students away from students of color, high turnover rates of teachers (particularly in high-poverty areas), the reduction of state and district incentives for teachers to get advanced degrees, the elimination of federal funds like Teaching American History grants, the intense politicization of debates about social studies curriculum content.

This excerpt from Katy's letter points to the many challenges our teachers are facing today. Powerful forces, such as the ones Katy mentions, are shaping our public schools and subsequently requiring teachers to deal with obstacles that are heavily related to the politics surrounding public education. Katy argues that one has to be not only knowledgeable about good teaching, but also equipped with the strategies and wherewithal to navigate these obstacles. As a teacher educator committed to social justice, she believes educators have a key role in creating a more peaceful and just society.

Although Katy foresees many obstacles for teachers entering the field, she also believes that the time for committed, passionate, critical, and justice-oriented people to enter the field has never been more important.

She advises that new teachers should "stay up" on disciplinary content and cutting-edge "best practices" in the field, and also be informed about debates and policies about schooling. She encourages teachers to think and be critical about whatever is given to them, including the CCSS. She asks teachers to closely examine the standards, appreciate what you can work with, and be critical of what might be harmful to yourself and your students. Ask questions such as, "Who gains from this policy? Who gets hurt? Who made the decision to do this? Who was left out of that decision making? How will this interact with the larger dynamics of school reform and education politics?"

Katy offers teachers a powerful suggestion. She believes that a socially just world relies on the hard work of teachers; however, she proposes that teachers remain informed about the debates and policies surrounding schooling. She argues that teachers need to critically examine the resources and tools given to them, including state and federal standards. Although Katy sees potential with the new standards, she advises teachers remain critical. Katy hopes teachers will continue to ask essential questions surrounding issues of power and bias in relation to the new standards.

Prevailing norms and practices in schools may make it difficult to integrate our visions of social justice. We may look to our colleagues for support, but may find ourselves unable to identify colleagues in our school with similar values. We may work to change the culture of our schools, and yet engaging in social justice work and educating others may feel isolating and tiresome. Restrictive policies, such as mandated curriculum, may confine us from teaching what we want to teach. As we work to restructure curriculum and disrupt the Eurocentric narrative portrayed in textbooks, we lean on outside resources to integrate the voices of those too often silenced and marginalized from the curriculum. These resources may be costly and time-consuming to find. We may also experience resistance from students and parents. Parents may disagree with what we are teaching in the classroom, and not want their students to engage in discussions that push back against the mainstream narrative that they were conditioned to believe is true.

In the effort to address these challenges, many of which deal with time, resources, and isolation, teachers must seek sources of support to sustain their social justice teaching. For most of the teachers in our study, they were able to promote their focus on social justice teaching by connecting with others who carried like-minded visions.

IMPORTANCE OF FINDING COMMUNITY

Teachers need professional networks to help them sustain and deepen their teaching practice (Achinstein & Ogawa, 2006; Sleeter, 2007). Isabel Morales, a social studies teacher at Los Angeles High School of the Arts, concurs with this statement. In her letter, she advises teachers to "connect with educators who inspire and support you, whether at your school site, at conferences, or online. They will be a great source of energy and strength when you need it most." Attempting to be the "lone ranger" (Wade, 2007, p. 94) of social justice at your school can feel tiresome and ineffective given the great institutional barriers you will be forced to confront. By creating professional networks, you will have the opportunity to collaborate with others as you reflect on your practice and grapple with the challenges you are facing in the classroom. Sleeter argues that "professional networks can help teachers navigate accountability demands without abandoning the theories and practices that they believe in" (2007, p. 28). Finding hope and possibility within a teaching context of standardization and accountability can feel especially daunting, especially for beginning teachers; a support network can provide the community you need to develop and sustain your work. Teachers can learn from others in their network ways in which to gain autonomy in the classroom.

Many of the teachers in this study pointed to the importance of having a professional network to help them sustain their commitment to teach for social justice, including Brian, who suggests teachers "seek out those who are like you, those who are justice-minded within your school and community." As a new teacher, taking on the challenge of teaching for social justice may often times require resisting restrictive policies. Achinstein and Ogawa (2006) advise that "those who wish to challenge the dominant system seek allies in a network of professional communities, where norms of inquiry and reflection are supported" (p. 60). Professional networks can help teachers to better take on the challenge of social justice work, as teachers can learn from their colleagues how to "teach against the grain" without putting their job on the line. The solidarity provided by a community of like-minded educators can also help teachers put forth a united front when they feel like your job might be in jeopardy. Your community can help you to navigate institutional challenges, such as push back from parents and administration, when attempting to enact curriculum that may conflict with the values supported by their school. Communities can also provide spaces for teachers to reflect on struggles in their classroom and school and discuss ways to move forward and take action. Additionally, justice-oriented teaching communities can also offer new teachers tips and helpful suggestions so that they may avoid burnout when teaching for social justice feels overwhelming and impossible in their current school settings, as it will be.

Most of the teachers in our study have witnessed and experienced challenges related to standards-based initiatives, especially through the era of NCLB. Seeking out justice-oriented teacher communities and professional networks as a strategy proved essential to them in sustaining and supporting their work. In this next section we share advice from our teacher participants. They each assert the importance of building a community of like-minded colleagues. We outline different support systems teachers may find helpful, including finding a mentor, a support network of teachers, a justice-oriented organization, or resources that provoke inspiration and learning.

MENTORSHIP

Mentorship is a key resource for anyone in any field and essential to our work as educators. Teaching is the only profession that requires novices to fulfill the same duties and responsibilities as their experienced colleagues (Tellez, 1992). Beginning teachers, oftentimes, are given difficult teaching loads, which might include no preparation periods, large classroom sizes, or assigned children which need/should have the best teachers and one-on-one support. In addition to learning the curriculum and establishing classroom management for the first time, new teachers must also find ways to integrate their visions of social justice into their practice. There is no textbook or concrete way of doing this. Mentors carry with them knowledge and expertise that cannot be replicated by any textbook or graduate-level course.

As mentors have been in the classroom for sometimes decades, they have seen the ebbs and flows of educational policy. They have experienced the pressures of standards-based reform, felt the challenges related to accountability and standardization, and suffered the consequences of each. And yet, they are still teaching. From our mentors, we can learn how to sustain our visions of social justice. We can also learn how to critically examine and navigate educational policy so that we can maintain our commitments to social justice teaching. Mentors' words of wisdom can also offer us hope and possibility when teaching for social justice seems impossible. Amelie Baker, a 9th- and 10th-grade history teacher, asserts the importance of finding a mentor or "elder" in the field. She explains in her letter,

> This elder may not do things the way you were taught in graduate school, they may not look like the elder you envisioned, but there only needs to be one truth, that this teacher is beloved by their students. In my first year of teaching, my elder was a petite southern implant with a blonde bob hairstyle and coral lipstick. She called all of her students "pollitos" or little chickens, maybe more along the line of chickadees. The students adored her and she managed to inspire and rally them to do things I had never imagined possible. These teachers will always be incredibly busy because in the later years of their career they will still be pushing themselves to try new techniques and bring new things to their students. I recommend learning how they take their coffee or what their favorite treat is and having it on hand when you need their advice. There will be times when simply their confirmation that you were doing right is the only thing that will get you through the day.

For Amelie, her mentor or "elder" offered her what graduate school could not, a window into the classroom of an experienced justice-oriented teacher who was doing the work she wanted to do. Although her mentor was busy, she found ways to connect with her by bringing in her favorite treats. Mentorship, to Amelie, was not just about having long conversations about lesson planning, but also simple confirmations that let her know that she was on the right path. As a mentor herself now, Amelie understands the importance of having an "elder." Mentors serve as experienced and trusted advisors that are there to support you. In her case, her mentor was there to give her "whatever she needed," whether it be constructive feedback on a lesson, help developing a unit, or ideas around classroom management issues.

Mentors may be difficult to find; thus, teachers may also find mentorship across distance and time. Education philosophers and theorists may provide teachers with the words of support and hopefulness they may be looking for to help sustain their teaching. Katy suggests publications like *Rethinking Schools,* blogs like Deborah Meier and Diane Ravitch's *Bridging Differences,* and books like Bree Picower's *Practice What You Teach: Social Justice Education in the Classroom and the Streets*. Other teachers shared the works of Paolo Freire and bell hooks as touchstone texts for their teaching.

BUILD A SUPPORT NETWORK OF TEACHERS

In addition to having a mentor, finding a justice-oriented teaching community is essential to sustaining and supporting one's work as a social justice educator. As social justice educators may often feel isolated in their visions for teaching, those committed to justice-oriented work may counter that isolation by finding a network of like-minded colleagues to surround themselves with (Henning, 2013). Amelie Baker, argues, "teaching can become very lonely and students are not our peers, we need other adults who face the same dilemmas we do." Critical inquiry groups can help support teachers' practice by providing teachers with a space to share resources and discuss ways social justice can be linked with classroom practices. For example, some social justice teacher organizations have formed inquiry to action groups (ItAGs), which are small groups of educators, parents, students, activists, teaching artists, and community members who meet to share experiences, dialogue about readings, exchange ideas, and develop plans of actions. The New York Collective of Radical Educators (NYCoRE) offers 8-week workshops/ItAGs cofacilitated by a teacher and another person who has knowledge on the topic. The ItAG is similar to a study group, in which the group inquiries into a particular topic and then works together to create action around their area of study. Similarly, the Teachers for Social Justice (TSJ) organization in Chicago recently launched their ItAGs. The goal of these ItAGs is to pursue a common inquiry on a social justice topic and create an action around this area of study. Collective spaces such as critical inquiry groups can serve as a network of support for new teachers. Teachers can dialogue about the issues their students are facing in the classroom, share relevant literature, and develop curriculum collaboratively based on the discussions (Picower, 2007).

Carolina Valdez, a current doctoral student at UCLA, reiterates the importance of having a support network:

> Build the support network of like-minded teachers that you need to sustain your teaching practice. It's easy to say that you will always be the radical teacher you set out to be, but after grinding within the dehumanizing beast that is public education for a few years, it begins to take its toll. It becomes easier to just teach the scripted curriculum provided, rather than take the time to build a critical curriculum each time new standards and curriculum are pushed on schools. It becomes easier to roll with punitive punishment in schools than to build transformative alternatives. It becomes easier to leave when the bell rings, than to stay after and make yourself available to students and parents.

As a veteran teacher, Carolina understands the importance of finding a network of teachers to sustain her practice. She points to an important aspect of teaching, the toll pressures related to standardization and accountability take on justice-oriented teachers. Carolina helps us to see that a vision for social justice teaching is not enough: one needs a network of like-minded teachers to help sustain and support their teaching practice. Teachers will face myriad pressures, expectations to teach a scripted curriculum, prepare students for high-stakes tests, and adhere to standards, all of which may conflict with one's social justice leanings. Without her colleagues to support her, Carolina may not have been the radical teacher she hoped to be. Carolina asserts that teaching for social justice is complex, demanding, and time-consuming, Carolina strongly advises novices entering the field to find a group of like-minded teachers to help support one's work.

Lyndsay Oakes, an 8th-grade history teacher in New York, shares a similar recommendation in her letter:

> Join or form a study group of two or more teachers to develop lesson plans, materials, or assessments; implement them in your classroom; and then reconvene to discuss results and next steps. Creating a social studies classroom in which students are engaged in historical thinking, reading, and writing about rich content is worth the effort.

Lyndsay found colleagues in the social studies departments of her school and district to collaborate with through a study group. To sustain her practice, she used the study group as a platform to help her create and enact justice-oriented social justice curriculum in the classroom.

Elizabeth Haims, a 15-year National Board Certified bilingual history teacher, gives novices the following advice:

> Find allies within the school or community. There are good people everywhere. Find them. Talk with them. You will need support when you feel down and not good enough. When taking on the system, if you choose to do so, do not do it alone. Have a team with you. Allies can be students, parents, other teachers, school workers, and even community members. Keep reaching out when you falter and you will find a career that gives you more than you ever knew possible.

Elizabeth strongly believes that we need to find allies to sustain our work as social justice educators. As we work with our network and communities, we can work to collectively change what we see as unjust in our schools and communities. Our allies will support us and help to lift us up when we feel hopeless in our work. As the other mentor teachers in this chapter advised finding like-minded colleagues to connect with, Elizabeth stresses that one's community can also consist of students, parents, community members, and other school workers in the district. Each of these members and groups can help to support and sustain your work.

As we work to create our communities, we do not have to limit ourselves to our schools and districts. Social media sites, such as Facebook, LinkedIn, and Instagram, give us the opportunities to learn with and from colleagues from all over the world. Through these spaces we can share ideas and gain support from like-minded colleagues.

JOINING ORGANIZATION/PROFESSIONAL NETWORKS

Organizations and professional networks also serve as a key component to sustaining our work as social justice educators. They help us to increase our understanding of social justice theory and content, and also provide us with a greater sense of community as we gain partnership with other justice-oriented educators. As Jennifer Shah explains, "those who are interested in teaching for social justice and cultivating a justice-oriented citizenry while implementing the Common Core should reach out to the larger professional community and create alliances with those doing the work successfully."

There are many justice-oriented networks available to help support teachers' conceptual and practical approaches to teaching for social justice. Some of these groups are formally affiliated with universities, beginning during and continuing beyond candidates' preservice experiences (e.g., Oakes & Rogers, 2006; Quartz, 2003; Ritchie, An, Cone, & Bullock, 2013). Others take the form of informal, unaffiliated inquiry groups, such as grassroots ItAGs hosted by NYCoRE in New York City, TSJ in Chicago, Teachers 4 Social Justice (T4SJ) in San Francisco, National Association of Multicultural Education (NAME), the Association of Raza Educators (ARE) in California, and justice-oriented teacher networks nationwide (see Network of Teacher Activist Groups at www.teacheractivistgroups.org). As mentioned above, these organizations can be a great place to form and organize a critical inquiry group, such as ItAGs, and/or receive professional development and build community. Membership into these organizations can also provide teachers with a network to participate in efforts to make social change and push back against unjust educational policy. For example, the National Association of Multicultural Education California chapter is a group of teachers, teacher educators, students, parents, and community members invested in creating socially just and equitable learning communities in California schools and classrooms.

As teaching for social justice can be isolating work, Katy Swalwell encourages teachers not to counter the isolation by closing their classroom door, but rather to find opportunities to connect with like-minded educators and groups. She explains in her letter,

> Stay informed about the bigger picture—and get involved. Join others who are organized and together take action against policies that you think are bad, directing civic engagement to the source of the problem while simultaneously negotiating the consequences in your own classroom so that students do not suffer.

By organizing and collaborating with others, we may be able to find ways to challenge what we see as unjust in our classrooms and schools. We may also be better able to uphold our commitment to teach for social justice as we have a community of educators to work with.

As Katy shares with us different outlets teachers can turn toward to help sustain their commitment to teach for social justice, she also points to an important aspect of justice-oriented work, the ability to stay hopeful. Part of being able to stay hopeful is to stay connected. Finding mentors you can lean on, resources that keep you inspired, and like-minded individuals and groups you can connect with are all pieces of sustaining our work as social justice educators and having a long-lived career in teaching.

CONCLUSION

Teachers are expected to teach in a context that is laden with challenges related to standardization and accountability. As new teachers, feelings of helplessness and loss of hope may be directly linked to one's desire to teach for social justice. Day-to-day challenges such as navigating mandated curriculum, managing the classroom, and preparing students for standardized tests are forced to take precedence as these may be the tasks that are valued by the administration. In consequence, teachers may struggle to find ways to enact their visions of social justice into practice.

The teachers highlighted in this chapter were each able to find ways to navigate challenges surrounding standardization and accountability to uphold their commitment to teach for social justice, but they did not do this alone. Each leaned on a community of like-minded educators to help support and sustain their work. They found mentors and organizations, sought out justice-oriented teachers in their schools and/or districts, reached out through social media, found inspiring resources, or joined professional networks as a means of enduring their work as social justice educators. Each of these resources provided different avenues of support, including access to justice-oriented lesson plans, validation for the work they were doing, a collective means of pushing back against unjust education policy, and a space to find support regardless of the challenges that they were dealing with in the classroom. In end, the role of justice-oriented teacher communities and professional networks proved to be an essential strategy for sustaining and supporting the teachers' work.

CHAPTER 8

Teaching as a Political Act

Teaching is an inherently political act. Every decision we make in the classroom—from the topics we prioritize to the texts we highlight to the pedagogy we employ—is in response to a politicized system that reflects a complex constellation of factors. Decades of racialized social policies, district lines, and funding matrices have led to gross disparities in educational opportunity and outcome across neighboring communities. These inequities have left urban districts especially vulnerable to neoliberal "reforms," including privatization, standardization, and increased testing (Lipman, 2011). As districts and states enter into lucrative contracts with private companies, thus inviting corporate influence into conversations about curriculum, assessment, and discipline, top-down reforms, like the CCSS, are implemented with little opportunity for input at the local level. Intense pressures toward accountability undermine both the teaching profession as a whole and individual teachers' ability to use their expertise to make instructional decisions (Lipman, 2011; Milner IV, 2013). Thus, schools are neither politically neutral nor "objective" environments, and thus everything that occurs within them is necessarily reflective of their politicized nature.

As a discipline, social studies is especially susceptible to political influence. The recent controversies regarding new textbooks in use in Texas offer a valuable case study of the practical impact of this influence. These textbooks, purchased for use by 5 million public school students, reflect Texas's revised history standards, which minimize historical and contemporary racism. The textbooks suggest that states' rights, rather than slavery, were the primary cause of the Civil War, and entirely omit discussion of the Ku Klux Klan and Jim Crow Laws (Brown & Brown, 2010). They also falsely amplify debates regarding human responsibility for climate change (National Center for Science Education, 2014), thus prioritizing the energy industry's economic interests over the expertise of the scientific community. While these issues would be concerning in and of themselves, as the second-largest textbook purchaser in the country, Texas's textbooks invariably affect those in other states, raising fears regarding their impact on the teaching of U.S. history nationwide (e.g., Brown & Brown, 2010). Moreover, they reflect a wider acknowledgment of the politicization of social studies curriculum, with even the most conservative reformers acknowledging that many state social studies standards "seeking to mold students to specific political outlooks rather than to encourage historical comprehension or independent critical thought" (Stern & Stern, 2011, p. 8).

While justice-oriented teachers can use case studies like these to foreground the opportunity to foster students' critical literacy skills by, for example, inviting them to compare how multiple textbooks address similar topics (see Agarwal-Rangnath, 2013), they are also illustrative of the intensely politicized context in which we teach. Teaching is not neutral, yet the myth of an objective, politically neutral curriculum remains a powerful force in education. Kevin Kumashiro (2008) refers to this as the myth of "common sense," in which a specific, culturally hegemonic set of curricula and practices are presumed to be the commonsensical, "normal" approach to schooling. Justice-oriented teaching is then "dismissed as biased or politically motivated, as a distraction from the real work of schools, as inappropriate for children, or as simply nonsensical" (p. 5). Kumashiro argues that the perpetuation of this belief is not accidental, but rather the result of a sophisticated, multifaceted strategy designed to preserve an educational system that privileges those in power.

However, rather than allowing their vision to be co-opted by this rhetoric, justice-oriented teachers see themselves as members of growing countermovement in which they work collectively with students, community members, teachers, and teacher educators to promote a more just educational system (Ritchie, 2012). They embrace their agency, reenvisioning themselves as cocreators of, rather than participants in, educational systems. Furman (2012) offers a useful framework for considering social justice leadership, suggesting that social justice leaders are "action oriented and transformative, committed and persistent, inclusive and democratic, relational and caring, reflective, and oriented toward a socially just pedagogy" (p. 195). This vision echoes the themes raised by teachers throughout this book, who advise new teachers to examine their beliefs about social justice, the implications of that vision for their curriculum and pedagogy, and then work in solidarity with students, colleagues, and the broader community to enact meaningful, systemic change.

In addition to embracing their agency, justice-oriented teachers also reframe the concept of accountability. Instead of thinking of themselves as primarily accountable to external mandates regarding curriculum and testing, they see accountability as a more complex constellation. Justice-oriented teachers consider themselves accountable to their students, their community, and their social justice vision. They rely on their mentors, professional learning communities, and relationships with students, teachers, and other local stakeholders to help them follow through on their commitment to justice. Finally, justice-oriented teachers resist educational policies and reforms that threaten to undermine their effectiveness in the classroom. They engage in local and national activism with and on behalf of their students and their profession, willing to take personal and professional risks rather than become complicit with inequitable systems.

In this chapter, we examine the ways justice-oriented teachers advocate for themselves and their students, drawing examples from the teachers profiled in this book and the wider educational community. Throughout, we grapple with the complexities inherent in teaching for social justice in a hostile system, including the risks and controversies that can push justice-oriented teachers out of the classrooms. We conclude the chapter by summarizing the steps that new teachers can take to prepare for, and sustain, careers as transformative educators.

EMBRACE AGENCY

The teachers in this book adopt stances of embracing, reframing, and resisting the CCSS and other educational mandates, depending on how those policies reflect their vision and the needs of their students. However, in addition to considering their response to external reforms, they also center their—and their students'—agency as they seek to enact justice. This isn't a simple task, and requires teachers to carefully consider ways to critically comply with and reflectively resist (Gorlewski, in press) unjust policies. As we consider how to use our position in the classroom to cultivate change, we must evaluate the ways our local contexts shape our approach.

Brian Gibbs, whom you first met in Chapter 2, illustrates this concept when referring to how he and his colleagues responded to an increase in standardized assessments in his school district:

> Prior to the CCSS, [Los Angeles Unified School District] attempted to implement periodic assessments. I had several friends outright refuse to give them. They just never showed up to get their boxes of tests or even if delivered refused to give them. I respect that but didn't think it was enough. I asked to see the principal and during this meeting outlined the themed and essential question-based curriculum and pedagogy I employed. I demonstrated how the curriculum was thematically aligned, built on itself, grew specific intellectual and academic skills for empowerment, how all the content necessary for the standardized tests was taught prior to it, and how the periodic assessment would interfere. My administrator understood but said he couldn't approve it alone, so I took several colleagues who were teaching similarly to meet with our area superintendent and then another higher-level group. Three weeks later we were able to opt out of the test. I'm not sure this could happen everywhere, but I do think that teachers don't ask enough questions, ask to meet one on one or prepare to defend the pedagogic and curricular choices they make.

In this excerpt, Brian touches on multiple factors that teachers must consider when embracing their agency. They must first evaluate whether there is a possibility for change: Brian refers to colleagues who refused to administer the tests rather than attempting to change the district assessment policy. They must evaluate the types of arguments most likely to enhance their impact: In this case, Brian drew on his principal's investment in standards-aligned, thematic, academically sophisticated curriculum that met the district-required outcome. And he engaged like-minded colleagues, taking strength in numbers as they interacted with increasingly powerful stakeholders. He insisted on his curricular and pedagogical expertise, refusing to allow a district mandate to define the breadth, scope, and form of his discipline.

Brian used his agency to shift assessment policy in his district. Isabel Morales, a founding social studies teacher at Los Angeles High School of the Arts, used hers to help build a teacher-led pilot school where teachers are given autonomy over budget, staffing, scheduling, curriculum, and governance. As part of a team of teachers, Isabel explored alternative school models, partnered with allies, and designed a pilot school proposal that was eventually approved by their school district. As Isabel argues, "when we are organized, we are powerful!" Seven years ago, they were one of two pilot schools in the school district—now there are nearly 50. Isabel explains that, "this change did not come from policymakers—it came from committed groups of teachers who wanted better educational opportunities for their students." By connecting with teachers, Isabel was able to design and create a school organized by teachers.

Isabel brings this commitment to agency and activism into her social studies classroom. One of her lessons, for example, was designed to help students challenge media portrayals that depicted them as "gangbangers and immigrants" who would vandalize their new, expensive school building:

> My students were outraged to hear these low expectations and stereotypes, and their anger motivated them to speak out. They researched the social context of their community, learning that a public high school had not been built in the area for almost 100 years. Students in their community, which has the highest population density in Los Angeles, were forced to attend overcrowded schools for generations. My students used their research to write thoughtful arguments in response to the negative press surrounding our school. They eagerly asked for their papers to be edited, saying, "I want to prove to those people that we deserve a good school and a good education." They posted their work online, inserting their voices into the public debate. This valuable lesson not only allowed students to build critical thinking, reading, and writing skills; it also facilitated the development of empowered identities, in which students stood up and defended their right to learn in inspiring, state-of-the-art facilities.

By modeling how students can engage in activism in response to personally and contextually relevant social issues, Isabel was able to integrate her commitment to social justice with the demands of teaching an academically rigorous social studies curriculum. Unlike some teachers, who might allow administrative mandates, a hostile climate, or pressures toward standardization to limit the scope of their activism (see Picower, 2012), Brian and Isabel drew on their assessment of localized needs to facilitate systemic change.

Similar emphases are woven throughout the literature on student- and teacher-led activism. Social studies teachers can use social action curriculum projects (Epstein, 2010, 2014; Schultz, 2008; Schultz & Baricovich, 2010; Schultz, McSurley, & Salguero, 2013), for example, to embody agency as they use justice-oriented curriculum to "exploit cracks" in accountability-driven systems (Schultz et al., 2013, p. 56). Like Isabel, teachers implementing social action curriculum projects follow their students' interests to help students "identify relevant and pressing issues . . . [and] work through possible solutions, which in turn provide chances for engagement in contingent action planning to solve their identified issue" (Schultz & Baricovich, 2010, p. 47). They then expand on students' initial inquiry to address key academic content and skills. In describing one such project, Schultz (2008) details his students' efforts to get a new school building to replace the crumbling, underfunded Chicago school they attended. While the district ultimately decided to close, rather than replace, their school, Schultz and his students gained local and national media attention for their advocacy and raised the specter of teacher—and student—agency as a viable political strategy. In addition to foregrounding his students' agency as cotheorizers and cocreators of curriculum, Schultz evidenced agency in his strategic response to administrative mandates. Like Brian and Isabel, he was responsive to local dynamics, so "instead of resisting the commonalities of lesson plans or scheduling routines . . . I complied with these requirements. I followed the rules, often going beyond the expectations in explanation and illustration" (p. 129). He documented ways his curriculum addressed state standards, and invited his administrator to visit his classroom regularly. These efforts enabled his principal to become an advocate for his practice, and allowed him to teach critically without risking his job.

This contextual reflexivity is a central consideration for justice-oriented teachers, as we seek to embody agency in authentic, meaningful ways that won't get us fired. In Brian's case, for example, he decided that using his agency to change assessment policy would be more effective than simple refusal; other teachers, in other contexts, might have responded differently (see below for discussion of the Opt Out movement as an example of teacher-led resistance). Teachers' approaches to agency invariably shift in response to their philosophy, social location, and evaluation of risk, as they select a strategy that best suits their unique circumstances (Priestly, Edwards, Priestley, & Miller, 2012). Prentice Chandler refers to this as "raging against the machine, quietly" as a new teacher in rural Alabama:

> I recognized early in my career that to teach about social justice issues in rural Alabama would be impossible if I made myself a target. I had to recognize *where I was,* and acknowledge that *going underground* with social justice was necessary (Chandler, 2006). I studied the state curriculum and found ways to integrate social justice oriented content into the state approved framework. In my role as "gatekeeper" (Thornton, 1991) I found chinks in the curricular armor, openings where I chose to allow the voices of the oppressed to speak on their own behalf.

In some moments, justice-oriented teaching is a loud process that brings public visibility to our work as part of a broader movement. In others, it's the subtle leverage of institutional power to enact local changes. Regardless of their approach, however, justice-oriented teachers must ask themselves what changes they hope to make, evaluate their unique resources and obstacles, and consider how they will work strategically to increase their impact.

Each of these examples highlights teachers using their location in the classroom to enact change in school curriculum, policy, or practice. However, these teachers also adopted very different approaches based on the unique needs, demands, and circumstances of their local community. Brian worked collaboratively with other teachers to advocate for policy changes that were undermining their autonomy. Isabel foregrounded students' own activism regarding local social issues, while Prentice "raged quietly" in response to the nuances of his school context. In so doing, each of these teachers demonstrates the importance of teacher agency as we strive to foster justice-oriented, rigorous, and engaging learning experiences for students. In addition to leveraging their professional expertise in the classroom, teachers can also use their agency to shift the conversation about education itself.

REFRAME ACCOUNTABILITY

The language of accountability is a driving force in contemporary schooling. Teachers are accountable to standards, testing schedules, and external mandates. Schools are accountable to state and federal metrics. With the implementation of value-added measures and merit-based pay schedules, test-based definitions of accountability will increasingly inform teachers' livelihood. However, despite the rhetoric of accountability, educational systems too often prioritize outside requirements over the localized needs of the communities they serve. State laws regarding standardized testing, for example, penalize schools that fail to meet score targets by withholding resources or punitively "taking over" the school by firing the teachers rather than engaging in a comprehensive examination of the factors affecting student performance.

Ladson-Billings (2006) drew attention to this misplaced construction of accountability in her presidential address at the American Educational Research Association (AERA) annual meeting. In this address, she urged educators to shift their focus from talking about the "achievement gap" to examining the "education debt" that the United States owes students, and especially students of color, who have been systematically denied access to adequate social, fiscal, and educational resources. Essentially, she argues that by focusing on the achievement of individual students, and racial correlations in that achievement, we minimize the breadth and longitudinal impact of deeply embedded systemic inequities. Despite the rhetoric of accountability, analyses that look only at differences in test scores rarely hold themselves accountable for identifying and enacting substantive solutions.

By contrast, justice-oriented teachers think holistically about the concept of accountability. In addition to their accountability for students' content learning (see Chapter 6), they also consider themselves accountable to their students' interests and evolving critical frameworks, to other teachers and community stakeholders, and to their own vision of justice. For many teachers, professional learning communities, like those highlighted in Chapter 7, offer a critical opportunity to hold themselves accountable. Tom Skjervheim, whom we first met in Chapter 2, described his transition from a school that "exacerbates the social, class, and racial inequities of our society" to one that promoted social justice. After years of "closing my door and remaining isolated professionally," he was relieved to find a school (City Arts and Technology High School in San Francisco) where he could learn "alongside teachers, leaders, students, and community members about how a school could truly challenge the inequities of our school and social system."

> At CAT I found the professional community I was looking for. We served some of San Francisco's most marginalized communities,

> and a predominantly under-privileged (1st generation college bound, eligible for free-reduced lunch) student population. I was immersed in a truly collaborative professional culture, and was consistently inspired by (and in awe of) incredibly talented, passionate, and dedicated educators. Most importantly, my peers at CAT deeply held the belief that we had a responsibility to hold all students to high standards, and an even greater responsibility to ensure all students reached those high standards.

For justice-oriented teachers, the concept of accountability extends beyond student test scores: It also includes teachers' ability to hold each other accountable to making difficult curricular and political decisions, continuing to participate in professional development, and building relationships with local communities.

While Tom was able to find this community in his own school, other teachers look outside their classrooms. In describing her participation in a professional learning community, Lindsay Oakes comments,

> I have found it helpful to engage in this work with colleagues in the social studies departments of my school and other schools in my district. If you have like-minded colleagues with whom you can collaborate, I encourage you to do so. Join or form a study group of two or more teachers to develop lesson plans, materials, or assessments; implement them in your classroom; and then reconvene to discuss results and next steps.

In Chapter 7, we described some of the ways justice-oriented teachers use inquiry groups and action research cycles to think collectively about critical issues in education. In the next section, we will examine how teachers move from inquiry to action as they use their learning to increase their impact.

COLLECTIVE ACTION FOR SOCIAL JUSTICE

As Isabel reflects on her efforts to promote justice in her district, she advises new teachers to consider how they can work in solidarity with others to increase their power:

> As you embark on your social justice teaching career, please remember that you are not alone. The overwhelming majority of teachers care about developing students who will become

> compassionate leaders and innovators, not excellent test-takers. . . . When I encounter teachers who are frustrated with their working conditions, I remind them that teachers have more power than we realize. I work at a teacher-led pilot school with autonomy over budget, staffing, scheduling, curriculum, and governance—and I love it. We were not, however, simply handed these autonomies. Our team of teachers worked hard to organize themselves, explore alternative school models, partner with allies, and design a pilot school proposal that would be approved by the school district. . . . This change did not come from policymakers—it came from committed groups of teachers who wanted better educational opportunities for their students. When we are organized, we are powerful!

This idea of collective action for social justice is a key element of conceptualizing social justice teaching as not only a practice, but a movement. In her letter, Katy highlights other examples of teacher-led, justice-oriented collective actions that can inspire new teachers:

> There are also several real world examples of teachers fighting for justice, like Seattle's Garfield High faculty that got rid of a standardized test or the teachers in Tucson who defended their Ethnic Studies curriculum. Read about them, reach out to them, and follow in their footsteps. In your career, there will likely be dozens of new initiatives or sets of standards like the Common Core that you are expected to implement. Some of them will be inherently strong and some will be inherently flawed, but all will be unfolding within a political context that you have to take into account. Stay hopeful, stay connected, and stay strong—and don't forget to give yourself a break every once in awhile so that you have the stamina to keep fighting the good fight.

Katy's advice to stay hopeful and stay connected reminds us that collective action not only increases our power, but also increases our ability to continue to advocate for justice over time. Finding mentors you can lean on, resources that keep you inspired, and like-minded individuals and groups you can connect with are all pieces of sustaining our work as social justice educators and having a long-lived career in teaching.

There are similar stories throughout the literature on collective actions for social justice, with the Opt Out movement among the most visible. What began as a series of small-scale, teacher and parent-led acts of resistance to standardized testing grew into a comprehensive movement with demonstrable implications for national education policy (see Hagopian, 2014; McDermott, Robertson, & Jensen, 2014). To date, hundreds of thousands of families nationwide have opted out of standardized tests in their states, leading policymakers to grapple with the implications of widespread resistance to educational mandates. Current iterations of the *Every Child Achieves Act* include provisions that the federal government cannot supersede state laws permitting children to refuse to take standardized tests. While it is not yet clear how federal education policy will reconcile this issue, it is a compelling case study in the power of collective action for social justice. It is also an opportunity to engage students in critically examining contemporary, contextually resonant activism: Organizations like the Chicago Grassroots Curriculum Taskforce have published curricular materials designed to support teachers in teaching about the Opt Out movement (available at grassrootscurriculum.org/opt-out-alternatives/), while collectives like FairTest (www.fairtest.org) and United Opt Out (unitedoptout.com) feature primary source texts and opportunities for student, teacher, and community engagement.

In addition to building local coalitions, justice-oriented teachers can also partner with existing action-oriented networks like the New York Collective of Radical Educators (NYCoRE), the National Association of Multicultural Education (NAME), or the Association of Raza Educators (ARE) to find like-minded colleagues (see Network of Teacher Activist Groups at www.teacheractivistgroups.org). In addition to reducing isolation, these groups host conferences and workshops to help teachers leverage their collective power to enact change. Membership into these organizations can also provide teachers with a network to participate in efforts to make social change and push back against unjust educational policy.

Nick and Ruchi, along with some of the teachers in this book, embodied this approach when working to institutionalize ethnic studies curriculum and mandated courses in California. They began by forming a local chapter of the National Association of Multicultural Education (CA-NAME) that focused specifically on creating social justice and equitable schools and classrooms in California. CA-NAME works to address state-level advocacy through coalition building and engaging in statewide education campaigns around equity in education. A primary focus of their efforts has been to support and advocate for ethnic studies in California. Nick and Ruchi, alongside a team of researchers, reviewed the extant research and published a paper supporting ethnic studies and its powerful potential to dramatically improve the academic learning and sense of empowerment of students of color, and that enacting ethnic studies pedagogy has implications for hiring and preparing teachers (Tintiangco-Cubales et al., 2015). This paper has been used as evidence to convince at last count 20 large and small school districts in California to institute plans to mandate ethnic studies courses as a high school graduation requirement for all of their students. It has also been used to hire, train, support, and evaluate ethnic studies teachers in those districts.

Teaching for social justice is a challenging endeavor, but working in solidarity enables us to increase our impact and sustain our spirits. As Elizabeth suggested in Chapter 7,

> Keep reaching out when you falter and you will find a career that gives you more than you ever knew possible.

Elizabeth, like so many of the teachers in this book, reminds us that our paths are long, and our opportunities for growth continual.

RESIST COMPLIANCE: ENTERING THE WORLD OF WARRIORS

As we come to the conclusion of this book, we consider the advice of the teachers who have walked and fought for social justice before us: Amelie Baker, Prentice Chandler, Eran DeSilva, Laura Einhorn, Nicole Lusiani Elliott, Dawn Fontaine, Brian Gibbs, Melissa Leigh Gibson, Elizabeth Haims, David Jauregui Jr., Jared Kushida, Sarah Lundy, Isabel Morales, Lindsay Oakes, Jennifer Shah, Tom Skjervheim, Katy Swalwell, Michael Swogger, Rory Tannebaum, and Carolina Valdez. Each of these teachers brings a unique perspective to this work, a perspective informed by their own philosophy, context, curricular priorities, and pedagogical approach.

Collectively, they present a compelling testimony to the breadth, depth, and rigor of justice-oriented approaches to teaching social studies.

These teachers don't necessarily approach the standards in the same way, or do so at all times. In some moments, they embrace the ways the CCSS's emphasis on critical literacy supports and validates examinations of traditionally marginalized historics. In others, they see them as an opportunity to reframe the nature of social studies itself, by centering contextually relevant investigations of historical and contemporary issues of social justice. And, at other times they resist the CCSS as part of a wider set of corporate reforms that undermine and destabilize public education in their classrooms and as a whole. In all cases, the teachers in this book demand—and embody—professional agency as they advocate with and on behalf of their students and communities. They work individually and collectively to expand their content-area expertise, create curricular resources, and implement pedagogy that reflects the imperative to enact justice within and despite the current educational climate.

Like all good historians, justice-oriented teachers seek to learn from the past and also to build on it. They learn to teach to their conscience, drawing strength from those who walk alongside them. This work is not easy, but there is strength in numbers. Collectively, they are building a movement of "warriors," working collectively to fight for students. In the words of Nicole,

> Thousands who came before you in this profession still serve students with the same verve and intention as they did when they were new teachers like you. Seek them out. You cannot emulate who they are because you are not them, but you can watch them—what they do, how they do it, and why—and use them as models for your own style. Most importantly, when the work gets hard, and it will, you will need them to take your hands, look you in the eye, and remind you why you must persist. . . .
>
> A *teacher*, Warrior. That's what you are. It's in your bones and it's in your heart. Persist, Warrior. Above all, persist. Keep learning every day. Ask yourself, everyday, *what did they teach me?* Because, believe it or not, they are likely teaching you more than you are teaching them.

We couldn't agree more. We are, ourselves, always learning from our students, from our communities, from our candidates, and from fellow teachers seeking ways to enact justice in challenging times. Together, we are warriors.

References

Achinstein, B., & Ogawa, R. (2006). (In)Fidelity: What the resistance of new teachers reveals about professional principles and prescriptive educational policies. *Harvard Educational Review, 76*(1), 30–63.

Agarwal, R. (2011). Negotiating visions of teaching: Teaching social studies for social justice. *Social Studies Research and Practice, 6*(3), 52–64.

Agarwal, R., Epstein, S., Oppenheim, R., Oyler, C., & Sonu, D. (2010). From ideal to practice and back again: Beginning teachers teaching for social justice. *Journal of Teacher Education, 61*(3), 237–247.

Agarwal-Rangnath, R. (2013). *Social studies, literacy, and social justice in the Common Core classroom.* New York, NY: Teachers College Press.

Au, W. (2009). Social studies, social justice: W(h)ither the social studies in high-stakes testing? *Teacher Education Quarterly, 36*(1), 43–58.

Au, W. (2013a). Coring social studies within corporate education reform: The Common Core State Standards, social justice, and the politics of knowledge in U.S. schools. *Critical Education, 4*(5).

Au, W. (2013b). What's a nice test like you doing in a place like this? The edTPA and corporate education "reform." *Rethinking Schools, 27*(4). Retrieved from www.rethinkingschools.org/archive/27_04/27_04_au.shtml

Ayers, W. (2001). *To teach: The journey of a teacher.* New York, NY: Teachers College Press.

Bartell, C. (2004). *Cultivating high-quality teaching through induction and mentoring.* Thousand Oaks, CA: Corwin Press.

Bieler, D. (2012). Possibilities for achieving social justice ends through standardized means. *Teacher Education Quarterly, 39*(3), 85–102.

Bigelow, B., & Peterson, B. (Eds.). (1998). *Rethinking Columbus: The next 500 years.* Milwaukee, WI: Rethinking Schools.

Bigelow, B., Harvey, B., Karp, S., & Miller, L. (Eds.). (2001). *Rethinking our classrooms: Teaching for equity and justice* (Volume 2). Milwaukee, WI: Rethinking Schools.

Brooks, J. G., & Dietz, M. E. (2012/13). The dangers and opportunities of the Common Core. *Educational Leadership, 70*(4), 64–67.

Brown, A., & Brown, K. (2010). Strange fruit indeed: Interrogating contemporary textbook representations of racial violence toward African Americans. *Teachers College Record, 112*(1), 31–67.

Brown, S. R. (2014, April 1). Parents oppose Common Core by pulling kids out of school day of exams. *New York Daily News*. Retrieved from www.nydailynews.com/new-york/education/parents-pull-kids-school-dodge-common-core-article-1.1742510

Cammarota, J., & Fine, M. (2008). *Revolutionizing education: Youth participatory action research in motion*. New York, NY: Routledge.

Chandler, P. (2006). Academic freedom: A teacher's struggle to include "Other" voices in history. *Social Education, 70*(6), 354–357.

Cochran-Smith, M. (1991). Learning to teach against the grain. *Harvard Educational Review, 61*(3), 279–310.

Cochran-Smith, M. (2000). Blind vision: Unlearning racism in teacher education. *Harvard Educational Review, 70*(2), 157–190.

Cochran-Smith, M. (2004). *Walking the road: Race, diversity, and social justice*. New York, NY: Teachers College Press.

Cochran-Smith, M. (2010). Toward a theory of teacher education for social justice. In A. Hargreaves et al. (Eds.), *Second international handbook of educational change* (pp. 445–467). Dordrecht, The Netherlands: Springer.

Cochran-Smith, M., Shakman, K., Jong, C., Terrell, D. G., Barnatt, J., & McQuillan, P. (2009). Good and just teaching: The case for social justice in teacher education. *American Journal of Education, 115*(3), 347–377.

Coffey, H. (2015). Critical literacy. *K–12 teaching and learning from the UNC School of Education*. Retrieved from www.learnnc.org/lp/pages/4437

Cuban, L. (1991). History of teaching in social studies. In J. P. Shaver (Ed.), *Handbook of research on social studies teaching and learning* (pp. 197–209). New York, NY: Macmillan.

Cushman, K. (2005). *Fires in the bathroom: Advice for teachers from high school students*. New York, NY: The New Press.

Delpit, L. (1988). The silenced dialogue: Power and pedagogy in educating other people's children. *Harvard Educational Review, 58*(3), 280–298.

Dover, A. G. (2009). Teaching for social justice and K–12 student outcomes: A conceptual framework and research review. *Equity & Excellence in Education, 42*(4), 506–524.

Dover, A. G. (2013a). Getting "up to code": Preparing for and confronting challenges when teaching for social justice in standards-based classrooms. *Action in Teacher Education, 35*(2), 89–102.

Dover, A. G. (2013b). Teaching for social justice: From conceptual frameworks to classroom practices. *Multicultural Perspectives, 15*(1), 3–11.

Dover, A. G. (2015). "Promoting acceptance" or "preparing warrior scholars": Variance in teaching for social justice vision and praxis. *Equity & Excellence in Education, 48*(3), 361–372.

Dover, A. G. (2016). Teaching for social justice and the Common Core: Justice-oriented curriculum for language arts and literacy. *Journal of Adolescent & Adult Literacy, 59*(6). Advance online version available at onlinelibrary.wiley.com/doi/10.1002/jaal.488/abstract

Duncan-Andrade, J. R. (2009). Note to educators: Hope required when growing roses in concrete. *Harvard Educational Review, 79*(2), 181–194.

Epstein, S. E. (2010). Activists and writers: Student expression in a social action literacy project. *Language Arts, 87*(5), 363–372.

Epstein, S. E. (2014). *Teaching civil literacy projects: Student engagement with social problems, grades 4–12*. New York, NY: Teachers College Press.

Evans, R. W. (2006). The social studies wars, now and then. *Social Education, 70*(5), 317–321.

Ferguson, D. (2013). Martin Luther King, Jr. and the Common Core: A critical reading of "close reading." *Rethinking Schools, 28*(2), 18–21.

Figueroa, A. (2013, August 6). 8 things you should know about corporations like Pearson that make huge profits from standardized tests. *Alternet*. Retrieved from www.alternet.org/education/corporations-profit-standardized-tests

Flores, M. T. (2007). Navigating contradictory communities of practice in learning to teach for social justice. *Anthropology & Education Quarterly, 38*(4), 380–402.

Freire, P. (1970). *Pedagogy of the oppressed*. New York, NY: Seabury.

Freire, P. (1974). *Education for critical consciousness*. New York, NY: Crossroad Publishing.

Furman, G. (2012). Social justice leadership as praxis: Developing capacities through preparation programs. *Educational Administration Quarterly, 48*(2), 191–229.

Gorlewski, J. (2015, April). Accountable to whom? Normalizing culturally sustainable assessment. Paper presented at the annual meeting of the American Educational Research Association, Chicago, IL.

Gorlewski, J. A. (In press). Foreword: Who decides and why it matters. In T. Gurl, L. Caraballo, L. Grey, J. H. Gunn, D. Gerwin, & H. Bembenutty (Eds.), *Privatization, policy, performance assessment, and professionalization: Affordances and constraints for teacher education programs*. New York, NY: Springer.

Gorski, P. (2010). The scholarship informing the practice: Multicultural teacher education philosophy and practice in the United States. *International Journal of Multicultural Education, 12*(2). Retrieved from ijme-journal.org/index.php/ijme/issue/view/16

Grant, C., & Sleeter, E. (2011). *Doing multicultural education for achievement and equity*. New York, NY: Taylor & Francis.

Grant, C. A., & Agosto, V. (2008). Teacher capacity and social justice in teacher education. In M. Cochran-Smith, S. Feiman-Nemser, D. J. McIntyre, & K. E. Demers (Eds.), *Handbook of research on teacher education: Enduring questions in changing contexts* (3rd ed., pp. 175–200). New York, NY: Routledge.

Haberman, M. (1995). *Star teachers of children in poverty*. West Lafayette, IN: Kappa Delta Pi.

Hagopian, J. (Ed.). (2014). *More than a score: The new uprising against high stakes testing*. Chicago, IL: Haymarket Books.

Henning, N. (2013). We make the road by walking together: New teachers and the collaborative and context-specific appropriation of shared social justice-oriented practices and concepts. *Teaching and Teacher Education, 36*, 121–131.

Heybach, J. A. (2009). Rescuing social justice in education: A critique of the NCATE controversy. *Philosophical Studies in Education, 40*, 234–245.

Horn, R. A. (2003). Developing a critical awareness of the hidden curriculum through media literacy. *The Clearinghouse, 76*(6), 298–300.

Hytten, K., & Bettez, S. C. (2011). Understanding education for social justice. *Educational Foundations, 25*(1–2), 7–24.

Johnson, E. C. (2007). Critical literacy and the social studies methods course: How preservice social studies teachers learn and teach for critical literacy. *Social Studies Research and Practice, 2*(2), 145–168.

Johnson, E. M. (2013, May 14). Seattle schools back down from standardized test after protests. *Reuters*. Retrieved from www.reuters.com/article/2013/05/14/us-usa-education-testing-idUSBRE94D18D20130514

Johnson, L., Oppenheim, R., & Suh, Y. J. (2009). "Would that be social justice?" A conceptual constellation of social justice curriculum in action. *New Educator, 5*(4), 294–311.

Karp, S. (2013). The problems with the Common Core. *Rethinking Schools, 28*(2), 10–17.

Kauffman, D., Johnson, S. M., Kardos, S. M., Liu, E., & Peske, H. G. (2002). "Lost at sea": New teachers' experiences with curriculum and assessment. *Teachers College Record, 104*(2), 273–300.

Kelly, D. M., & Brandes, G. M. (2001). Shifting out of "neutral": Beginning teachers' struggles with teaching for social justice. *Canadian Journal of Education, 26*(4), 437–454.

Kimmel, L. (2014). *A taste of freedom: Gandhi and the great salt march.* New York, NY: Walkers Books.

Kumashiro, K. (2008). *The seduction of common sense: How the right has framed the debate on America's schools.* New York, NY: Teachers College Press.

Kumashiro, K. (2015). *Against common sense: Teaching and learning toward social justice.* New York, NY: Routledge.

Ladson-Billings, G. (1994). *The dreamkeepers: Successful teachers for African-American children*. San Francisco, CA: Jossey-Bass.

Ladson-Billings, G. (1995). But that's just good teaching! The case for culturally relevant pedagogy. *Theory into Practice, 34*(3), 159–165.

Ladson-Billings, G. (2006). From the achievement gap to the education debt: Understanding achievement in U.S. schools. *Educational Researcher, 35*(7), 3–12.

Leahey, C. (2013). Catch-22 and the paradox of teaching in the age of accountability. *Critical Education, 4*(6), 1–19.

Lee, E., Menkart, D., & Okaazawa-Rey, M. (Eds.). (2006). *Beyond heroes and holidays: A practical guide to K–12 anti-racist, multicultural education and staff development.* Washington, DC: Teaching for Change.

Lipman, P. (2011). Neoliberal urbanism, race, and urban school reform. In W. H. Watkins (Ed.), *The assault on public education: Confronting the politics of corporate school reform* (pp. 33–54). New York, NY: Teachers College Press.

Loewen, J. (2007). *Lies my teacher told me. Everything your American history textbooks got wrong*. New York, NY: Simon & Schuster.

Maguth, B. (2012). In defense of the social studies: Social studies programs in STEM education. *Social Studies Research and Practice, 7*(2), 65–90.

Marker, G., & Mehlinger, H. (1992). Social studies. In P. W. Jackson (Ed.), *Handbook of research on curriculum* (pp. 830–851). New York, NY: Macmillan.

Marker, P. M. (2006). The future is now: Social studies in the world of 2056. In E. W. Ross (Ed.), *The social studies curriculum: Purposes, problems, and possibilities* (3rd ed., pp. 77–96). Albany, NY: State University of New York Press.

Massey, D. (2004). "You teach!": Beginning teachers' challenges to teacher educators. *Reading Research and Instruction, 43*(4), 75–94.

McDermott, M., Robertson, P., & Jensen, R. (Eds.). (2014). *An activist handbook for the education revolution: United Opt Out's test of courage.* Charlotte, NC: Information Age.

Miller, S., (2010). Introduction: Teaching social justice. In S. Miller & D. Kirkland (Eds.), *Change matters: Qualitative research ideas for moving social justice theory to policy* (pp. 1–18). New York, NY: Peter Lang.

Miller, S., Beliveau, L., DeStigter, T., Kirkland, D., & Rice, P. (2008). *Narratives of social justice teaching: How English teachers negotiate theory and practice between preservice and inservice spaces*. New York, NY: Peter Lang.

Milner, R., IV. (2013). Scripted and narrowed curriculum reform in urban schools. *Urban Education, 48*(2), 163–170.

Murrell, P. C., Jr. (2001). *The community teacher: A new framework for effective urban teaching*. New York, NY: Teachers College Press.

National Center for Science Education. (2014). *Analysis of climate change in proposed social studies textbooks for Texas public schools.* Oakland, CA: Author. Retrieved from ncse.com/files/Texas-social-studies-report-2014.pdf

National Commission on Excellence in Education (NCEE). (1983). *A nation at risk: The imperative for educational reform.* Washington, DC: Author. Retrieved from www.ed.gov/pubs/NatAtRisk/index.html

National Council for the Social Studies. (2010). *National curriculum standards for social studies*. Silver Spring, MD: Author.

National Governors Association Center for Best Practices & Council of Chief State School Officers. (2010). *Common Core State Standards for English language arts and literacy in history/social studies, science, and technical subjects.* Washington, DC: Authors.

Nieto, S. (2000). *Affirming diversity: The sociopolitical context of multicultural education*. New York, NY: Longman.

North, C. (2006). More than words? Delving into the substantive meaning(s) of "social justice" in education. *Review of Educational Research, 76*(4), 507–535.

North, C. (2008). What is all this talk about "social justice?" Mapping the terrain of education's latest catchphrase. *Teachers College Record, 110*(6), 1192–1206.

Oakes, J., & Lipton, M. (2003). *Teaching to change the world* (2nd ed.). New York, NY: McGraw-Hill.

Oakes, J., & Rogers, J. (2006). *Learning power: Organizing for education and justice*. New York, NY: Teachers College Press.

Papola, A. (2013, Winter). Critical literacy, common core, and close reading. *Colorado Reading Journal*, 46–50.

Picower, B. (2007). Supporting new educators to teach for social justice: The critical inquiry project model. Penn GSE Perspectives in Urban Education, 5(1).

Picower, B. (2011). Resisting compliance: Learning to teach for social justice in a neoliberal context. *Teachers College Record, 113*(5), 1105–1134.

Picower, B. (2012). *Practice what you teach: Social justice education in the classroom and the streets*. New York, NY: Routledge.

Poplin, M., & Rivera, J. (2005). Merging social justice and accountability: Educating highly qualified, responsible and effective teachers. *Theory Into Practice, 44*(1), 27–37.

Powers, E. (2006, June 6). A spirited disposition debate. *Inside Higher Ed*. Retrieved from www.insidehighered.com/news/2006/06/06/disposition

Priestley, M., Edwards, R., Priestley, A., & Miller, K. (2012). Teacher agency in curriculum making: Agents of change and spaces for manoeuvre. *Curriculum Inquiry, 42*(2), 191–214.

Quartz, K. H. (2003). Too angry to leave: Supporting new teachers' commitment to transform urban schools. *Journal of Teacher Education, 54*(2), 99–111.

Ravitch, D. (2013). *Reign of error: The hoax of the privatization movement and the danger to America's public schools*. New York, NY: Knopf.

Ritchie, S. (2012). Incubating and sustaining: How teacher networks enable and support social justice education. *Journal of Teacher Education, 63*(2), 120–131.

Ritchie, S., An, S., Cone, N., & Bullock, P. (2013). Teacher education for social change: Transforming a content methods course block. *Current Issues in Comparative Education, 15*(2), 63–83.

Ross, E. W. (Ed.). (2014). *The social studies curriculum: Purposes, problems, and possibilities*. Albany, NY: State University of New York Press.

Ross, E. W., Mathison, S., & Vinson, K. D. (2014). Social studies education and standards-based education reform in North America: Curriculum standardization, high-stakes testing, and resistance. *Revista Latinoamerica de Estudios Educativos, 1*(10), 19–48.

Rubin, B. (2011). *Making citizens: Transforming civic learning for diverse social studies classrooms*. New York, NY: Routledge.

Rubin, B. (2015). A time for social studies: Talking with young people about Ferguson and Staten Island. *Social Education, 79*(1), 22–29.

Sambell, K., & McDowell, L. (1998). The construction of the hidden curriculum: Messages and meanings in the assessment of student learning. *Assessment and Evaluation in Higher Education, 23*(4), 391–402.

Schneider, M. (2015). *Common Core dilemma: Who owns our schools?* New York, NY: Teachers College Press.

Schultz, B. D. (2008). *Spectacular things happened along the way: Lessons from an urban classroom.* New York, NY: Teachers College Press.

Schultz, B. D., & Baricovich, J. E. (2010). Curriculum in the making: Theory, practice, and social action curriculum projects. *Journal of Curriculum Theorizing, 26*(2), 46–61.

Schultz, B. D., McSurley, J., & Salguero, M. (2013). Teaching in the cracks: Student engagement through Social Action Curriculum Projects. *International Journal of Critical Pedagogy, 4*(2), 53–68.

Sizer, T. (1992). *Horace's school: Redesigning the American high school.* Boston, MA: Houghton-Mifflin.

Sleeter, C., & Grant, C. (2007). *Making choices for multicultural education: Five approaches to race, class and gender* (6th ed.). New York, NY: John Wiley & Sons.

Sleeter, C., & Grant, C. (2011). Race, class, gender, and disability in current textbooks. In E. Provenzo Jr., A. N. Shaver, & M. Bello (Eds.), *The textbook as discourse: Sociocultural dimensions of American schoolbooks* (pp. 183–215). New York, NY: Routledge.

Sleeter, C. E. (2005). *Un-standardizing curriculum: Multicultural teaching in standards-based classrooms.* New York, NY: Teachers College Press.

Sleeter, C. E. (2007). Preparing teachers for multiracial and historically underserved schools. In G. Orfield & E. Frankenburg (Eds.), *Lessons in integration: Realizing the promise of racial diversity in America's schools* (pp. 171–198). Charlottesville, VA: University of Virginia Press.

Sleeter, C. E. (2011). *The academic and social value of Ethnic Studies: A research review.* Washington, DC: National Education Association.

Stern, S. M., & Stern, J. A. (2011). *The state of state U.S. history standards 2011.* Washington, DC: Thomas B. Fordham Institute. Retrieved from edexcellence.net/publications/the-state-of-state-us.html

Takaki, R. (2008). *A different mirror: A history of multicultural America.* Boston, MA: Back Bay Books.

Tellez, K. (1992). Mentors by choice, not design: Help-seeking by beginning teachers. *Journal of Teacher Education, 43*(3), 214–221.

Thieman, G., & Leski, S. (2015). Preparing secondary social studies teacher candidates to address Common Core State Standards and the C3 Framework with diverse learners. *Oregon Journal of the Social Studies, 3*(1), 13–32.

Thornton, S. J. (1991). Teacher as curricular-instructional gatekeeper in social studies. In J. Shaver (Ed.), *Handbook of research on social studies teaching and learning* (pp. 237–248). New York, NY: Macmillan.

Tintiangco-Cubales, A., Kohli, R., Sacramento, J., Henning, N., Agarwal-Rangnath, R., & Sleeter, C. (2015). Toward an Ethnic Studies pedagogy: Implications for K–12 schools from the research. *Urban Review, 47*(1), 104–125.

UCLA TEP Student Development Committee. (2002). Multiple pathways: Examining how students develop as transformative urban educators. In *Teaching for social justice: The successes and challenges of preparing urban educators (Year 1 Reports & Instructional Case Narratives of the Urban Teacher Education Collaborative)*. Los Angeles: UCLA Center X and the UCLA Institute for Democracy, Education & Access. Unpublished reports. [Co-authors: Burstein, J., Calahan, H., Dwyer, L., Furumoto, R., Howard, T., Joseph, R., Lane, S., Metcalfe, E. L., Olsen, B., Perez, M., & Swanson, I.].

Ujifusa, A. (2014, June 6). Days apart, two states opt to replace Common Core. *Education Week*. Retrieved from www.edweek.org/ew/articles/2014/06/06/35commonore.h33.html

van Hover, S. D., & Yeager, E. A. (2004). Challenges facing beginning history teachers: An exploratory study. *International Journal of Social Education, 19*(1), 8–21.

Virtue, D. C., Buchanan, A., & Vogler, K. E. (2012). Digging postholes adds depth and authenticity to a shallow curriculum. *Social Studies, 103*(6), 247–251.

Wade, R. (2001). Social action in the social studies: From the ideal to the real. *Theory into Practice, 40*(1), 23–28.

Wade, R. (2007). *Social studies for social justice: Teaching strategies for the elementary classroom*. New York, NY: Teachers College Press.

Westheimer, J., & Kahne, J. (2004). What kind of citizen?: The politics of educating for democracy. *American Educational Research Journal, 41*(2), 237–269.

Wiesel, E., & Wiesel, M. (2006). *Night*. New York, NY: Hill and Wang.

Wineburg, S. (1991a). Historical problem solving: A study of the cognitive processes used in the evaluation of documentary and pictorial evidence. *Journal of Educational Psychology, 83*, 73–87.

Wineburg, S. (1991b). On the reading of historical texts: Notes on the breach between school and academy. *American Educational Research Journal, 28*, 495–519.

Wineburg, S. (2010). Thinking like an historian. *Teaching with Primary Sources Quarterly, 3*(1), 2–4.

Wineburg, S., Martin, D., & Monte-Sano, C. (2011). *Reading like a historian: Teaching literacy in middle and high school history classrooms*. New York, NY: Teachers College Press.

Wolk, S. (2003). Teaching for critical literacy in social studies. *Social Studies, 94*(3), 101–106.

Young, I. M. (2006). Education in the context of structural injustice: A symposium response. *Educational Philosophy and Theory, 38*(1), 93–103.

Zeichner, K. (2003). The adequacies and inadequacies of three current strategies to recruit, prepare, and retain the best teachers for all students. *Teachers College Record, 105*(3), 490–515.

Zeichner, K. M., & Flessner, R. (2009). Educating teachers for social justice. In K. Zeichner (Ed.), *Teacher education and the struggle for social justice* (pp. 24–43). New York, NY: Routledge.

Zinn, H. (2002). *You can't be neutral on a moving train: A personal history of our times.* Boston, MA: Beacon Press.

Zinn, H. (2003). *A people's history of the United States.* New York, NY: HarperCollins.

Zollers, N., Albert, L. R., & Cochran-Smith, M. (2000). Pursuing social justice as a teacher education faculty: Collaborative dialogue, collaborative research. *Action in Teacher Education, 22*(2), 1–14.

Index

About the Teachers

To learn more about these teachers, and read their complete letters, visit our website: www.socialstudiesforsocialjustice.com

Amelie Baker has been working with, teaching, and learning from teenagers for 10 years in Boston, Massachusetts. She now mentors new teachers, which enables her to refine her passion and practice. She is inspired by teens and particularly their willingness to take risks. She was introduced to the radical history and future possibilities of education at Eugene Lang College at the New School through the extraordinary guidance of professor Gregory Tewksbury, leading her to be certain that education is humanity's best chance at redemption and achieving social justice. She is happy to be contacted at ms.baker1@gmail.com.

Dr. Prentice T. Chandler taught middle and secondary social studies for 5 years in Alabama public schools and is currently the coordinator of secondary education and associate professor of social studies education at the University of Cincinnati. His recent book, *Doing Race in Social Studies: Critical Perspectives* (2015), examines Critical Race Theory applications in social studies teaching and learning. In 2007, Dr. Chandler was named the Defense of Academic Freedom Award winner from the National Council for the Social Studies (NCSS) for his efforts teaching alternative history in Alabama public schools (2001–2006).

Eran DeSilva has 16 years of experience as an educator. Currently she teaches social studies and is the director of faculty professional development at Notre Dame High School, San Jose. She earned a double major from UC Davis in international relations and art studio and a master's in teaching from the University of San Francisco. She also enjoys working collaboratively with other educators as a colleague and a coach. Eran can be contacted at edesilva@ndsj.org.

Laura Einhorn is currently a member of a team founding an innovative and community-based K–12 school in Oakland, California. Previously, she taught high school history, "Race, Class, Gender, and Sexuality," and dance. Before finding her passion for social justice education, she interned at the Carr Center for Human Rights at Harvard University and was a staff member at the Tobin Project in Cambridge, Massachusetts.

Nicole Lusiani Elliott serves as a professional development instructor and instructional coach for history for the Hollyhock Fellowship, housed in the Center to Support Excellence in Teaching at Stanford University. In that role she implements summertime professional development for the history fellows and provides coaching support for them throughout the year. In addition to working for CSET, Nicole serves as an instructional coach and workshop presenter for the Center for Culturally and Linguistically Responsive Teaching and Learning, a nonprofit organization dedicated to improving the academic experience for underserved students. Prior to working for CSET and CLRTL, Nicole spent 20 years teaching at a high-needs East Bay public high school in California.

Dawn Fontaine has had 19 rewarding years educating young people in urban districts in Massachusetts. Over her career she sought out opportunities to impact more students by mentoring and coaching teachers in the hopes that they will develop increased efficacy that will transfer to student success. She made the decision to earn her master's degree in literacy because that is what she believed would benefit her students more than knowing more history. It also aligned with her thinking that standards are only outlining what to teach, not how to teach. Dawn is currently finishing her doctoral degree in teacher education and school improvement at the University of Massachusetts, Amherst.

Brian C. Gibbs taught history and American government at Theodore Roosevelt High School in East Los Angeles for 16 years. Currently a non-practicing history teacher, he is an assistant professor of education at the University of North Carolina at Chapel Hill.

Melissa Leigh Gibson taught social studies and English to grades 6–12 in both private and public schools in Chicago, Los Angeles, Wisconsin, and Guadalajara, Mexico. In addition, Melissa has led service learning programs for high school students with Northwestern University's Civic Education Project. Currently, she is an assistant professor in the Department of Education Policy & Leadership at Marquette University, where she prepares preservice teachers to be critical social studies educators. Her research is focused on disrupting educational inequity through justice-oriented and democratic pedagogies and policy. Melissa can be contacted at melissa.gibson@marquette.edu.

Elizabeth Haims is a 17-year, Nationally Board Certified, bilingual teacher who taught world and U.S. history for 10 years at Los Angeles High School, 2 years in Sierra Vista, Arizona, and 3 years in Pensacola, Florida. She currently teaches economics for Florida Virtual School. While in Los Angeles, she worked with the Coalition for Educational Justice (CEJ) organizing parents, teachers, and students for a more just school system.

David Jauregui Jr. has 12 years of experience teaching 7th–12th-grade social science in the cities of La Puente, Alhambra, and Oakland. Throughout his career, he has codeveloped creative curriculum, implementing simulations, seminars, and media analysis in his courses with an emphasis on critical thinking and deeper learning. He was also a member of the Facing History and Ourselves Teacher Leadership Team in Los Angeles. He has worked as a mentor teacher, a union representative, and an advocate for addressing systemic inequities, specifically pertaining to equitable course offerings. He gives a yearly talk for the Cal State LA teacher education program, and has coached swimming and water polo. He steps in and plays the upright bass with the school jazz band from time to time.

Jared Kushida is a dedicated and passionate social studies teacher of 10 years. He started his career at Azusa High School in Azusa, California, where he spent 4 years learning the craft of teaching. He then moved up to the Bay Area to join the 2nd-year staff at KIPP King Collegiate High School, a charter school in San Lorenzo (between Oakland and Hayward). Jared has designed the curriculum for U.S. History and War & Peace from scratch, and he continues to overhaul and innovate on every aspect of these courses. Progressive and critical education means everything to Jared, as do his students, to whom he owes all his respect and love!

Sarah Lundy currently serves as the director of teacher development for the Instructional Services Department at the Sonoma County Office of Education. Sarah's work is guided by a commitment to offering all students rigorous academic skill development alongside educational experiences that are highly relevant for their 21st-century lives. Sarah's interest in teacher education evolved from over a decade spent teaching academically vulnerable high school and middle school students in both Arizona and Oregon. Sarah taught K–12 teacher candidates and graduate students as a faculty member of Portland State University's Graduate School of Education and served as a Teaching & Research Fellow for the Choices Program for the 21st Century at Brown University. Sarah holds a B.A. in international relations from Gonzaga University, a M.A. in political science from the University of Arizona, and an Ed.D. in educational leadership and policy from Portland State University.

Isabel Morales is a proud product of Boyle Heights and the Los Angeles Unified School District. She holds a B.A. and M.Ed. from UCLA and is in her 11th year of teaching social studies at Los Angeles High School of the Arts. Isabel has traveled to Brazil, Costa Rica, and Mexico as the recipient of various educator fellowships. She was selected as a finalist for California Teacher of the Year, after being recognized as an LAUSD and Los Angeles County Teacher of the Year. She recently earned her Ed.D. from the University of Southern California.

Lindsay Oakes has taught social studies in a middle school in New York City public schools, where she has also served as an instructional coach, mentored new teachers, facilitated professional development workshops, taught creative writing, coached the ballroom dance team, and advised various extracurricular activities. She has participated in two Teaching American History grants, developed curricula for schools and cultural institutions in New York City, and taught graduate courses in disciplinary literacies for preservice and in-service teachers. She earned graduate degrees from Teachers College, Columbia University in teaching social studies and curriculum and teaching, as well as a certificate in school leadership from Baruch College (CUNY).

Jennifer K. Shah taught middle school social studies for 7 years in Chicago and is now teaching as adjunct faculty at Loyola University, working with teacher candidates at the undergraduate and graduate levels. Jennifer is currently completing her dissertation regarding critical literacy in the classroom and loves her interaction with the next generation of teachers. Her philosophy of social studies education involves culturally relevant pedagogy and teaching toward social justice. She can be contacted at jennybshah@gmail.com.

Tom Skjervheim took a nonprofit job out of the classroom to support the transformation of (predominantly urban) public school districts after 7 years of teaching history in high school classrooms. Over the past 4 years he has had the privilege of learning from dedicated and inspiring teachers and school/district leaders from across the nation. In the 2016–2017 school year, Tom is excited about returning to a high school community driven by social justice in Oakland, California.

Katy Swalwell is an assistant professor in the School of Education at Iowa State University. Her research focuses on social studies and social justice education, with a special emphasis on issues related to social class. Her book, *Educating Activist Allies: Social Justice Pedagogy with the Suburban and Urban Elite*, examines social justice history classes taught at elite high schools. She has been a Zinn Education Project Research Fellow and serves on the boards of the Social Studies and the Critical Educators for Social Justice special interest groups within the American Educational Research Association. She can be contacted at swalwell@iastate.edu or katyswalwell.com.

Michael J. Swogger taught high school American history and government for 13 years in south-central Pennsylvania and has been at Penn State Harrisburg teaching social studies methods since 2009. He also supervises social studies teacher candidates during their student teaching experience. He is currently a doctoral candidate in curriculum and instruction at Indiana University of Pennsylvania, focusing on teaching about race, social and cultural issues in education, and social studies/history education.

Rory P. Tannebaum is an assistant professor of education in social studies and history at Merrimack College in Boston, Massachusetts. He is a former middle school social studies teacher and graduate student of the University of Georgia and Clemson University. His research interests include the development of reform-oriented preservice social studies teachers and the use of discussion in the social studies classroom. He can be contacted at TannebaumR@merrimack.edu.

Carolina Valdez taught in the elementary grades in the Los Angeles Unified School District for 8 years while completing her Ph.D. in Urban Schooling at the University of California, Los Angeles. Carolina organized in Los Angeles several grassroots organizations, and helped found the People's Education Movement (People's Ed) in 2012, a decolonial organization for teachers of color (www.peoplesed.org). Now an assistant professor at California State University, Monterey Bay, Carolina prepares elementary educators for social justice teaching and continues to support the development of People's Ed chapters across the nation.

ABOUT THE SOCIAL JUSTICE EDUCATOR AND ARTIST

Luis-Genaro Garcia is a Los Angeles artist and high school art teacher in South Central Los Angeles currently pursuing a Ph.D. in Education at Claremont Graduate University. Drawing from his background in education, public art, and activism, he teaches art through a social justice curriculum that accounts for the ethnic, personal, and historical experiences of working-class Students of Color, in order to challenge the racist institutional barriers that exist for them.

About the Authors

Ruchi Agarwal-Rangnath is vice president of the National Association of Multicultural Education, California chapter. A former elementary education teacher, Ruchi's teaching and research focus is primarily on social studies education, teacher education for social justice, and multicultural education. Ruchi loves to hike, read, and spend time with her family. She recently published *Social Studies, Literacy, and Social Justice in the Common Core Classroom: A Guide for Teachers* (Teachers College Press, 2013) and articles in *Social Studies Research and Practice* and *The Urban Review*. Learn more about Ruchi's work at www.ruchirangnath.com.

Alison G. Dover is an assistant professor in the Department of Educational Inquiry and Curriculum Studies at Northeastern Illinois University. A former urban secondary English language arts teacher, Alison's scholarship examines approaches to teaching for social justice within and despite accountability-driven P–12 and teacher preparatory contexts. When she's not chasing after her spitfire daughters (ages 2 and 5), Alison spends her time writing. Her work has recently been published in *Teachers College Record*, the *Journal of Adolescent & Adult Literacy, Action in Teacher Education, Equity & Excellence in Education*, and *Multicultural Perspectives*. Learn more about Alison's work at www.alisongdover.com.

Nick Henning is an associate professor in the Department of Secondary Education at California State University–Fullerton (CSUF). A former urban secondary social studies teacher, coach, and daycare/afterschool program coordinator in the cities of Los Angeles and Minneapolis, Nick's present teaching and research focus on effective urban classroom teaching, social justice education, teacher education for social justice, social studies teaching and teacher education, and the creation of high-quality collaborative supports for social justice educators. He has been a teacher educator for 14 years in the teacher education programs of UCLA, Claremont Graduate University, and CSUF, and he is as passionate about soccer as he is about teaching. Dr. Henning's recent publications include articles in *Teaching and Teacher Education* and *The Urban Review.*